ISBN 978-1-331-75972-0
PIBN 10230970

1 MONTH OF
FREE
READING

at

www.ForgottenBooks.com

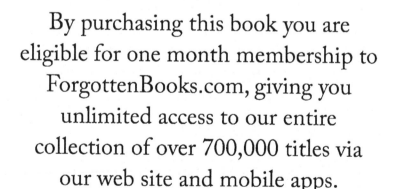

By purchasing this book you are eligible for one month membership to ForgottenBooks.com, giving you unlimited access to our entire collection of over 700,000 titles via our web site and mobile apps.

To claim your free month visit:

www.forgottenbooks.com/free230970

English
Français
Deutsche
Italiano
Español
Português

www.forgottenbooks.com

Mythology Photography **Fiction**
Fishing Christianity **Art** Cooking
Essays Buddhism Freemasonry
Medicine **Biology** Music **Ancient**
Egypt Evolution Carpentry Physics
Dance Geology **Mathematics** Fitness
Shakespeare **Folklore** Yoga Marketing
Confidence Immortality Biographies
Poetry **Psychology** Witchcraft
Electronics Chemistry History **Law**
Accounting **Philosophy** Anthropology
Alchemy Drama Quantum Mechanics
Atheism Sexual Health **Ancient History**
Entrepreneurship Languages Sport
Paleontology Needlework Islam
Metaphysics Investment Archaeology
Parenting Statistics Criminology
Motivational

AN

ENGLISH VERSION

(the original crowned by the French Academy)

OF

Mr FRÉDÉRIC MISTRAL'S

MIRÈIO

FROM THE ORIGINAL PROVENÇAL

UNDER THE AUTHOR'S SANCTION

AVIGNON		PARIS
J. ROUMANILLE, Libraire-Éditeur.		A. & W. GALIGNANI, rue de Rivoli.
MARSEILLE		NICE
CAMOIN, Libraire.		VISCONTI, Libraire.

AVIGNON, DECEMBER,

1867

PREFACE.

THE original of this work was published by
the author, M^r. Frédéric Mistral, in Septem-
ber 1859, and his fourth edition appeared
within three years after. He has since been
engaged on another, entitled *Calendau*, which
came out in January last, and has been re-
viewed by the Paris press with perhaps equal
praise, though certainly not the enthusiasm
with which *Mirèio* was greeted. The *Revue
des deux mondes* of the 1st April of this year
with reference to *Mirèio* says :

« Our readers will not have forgotten the
sensation excited by M^r. Frédéric Mistral's
Mirèio some eight years ago. *** It was greeted
with tumultuous applause. It was primitive
poesy! It was inspiration from the fountain

head! *** Ah! certes if we examine M^r. Mis-
tral's work carefully, how many skilful com-
binations, what ingenious artifices, do we not
discover! His originality however consists not
in these: an industrious arranger he is, and a
philological poet; but besides he has verily the
sense of things primitive, a taste for the simple
and the grand. The nature of which he imbi-
bed the milk was a strong one evidently [1], and
his heroes who are shepherds, cattle-breakers
and branders, keepers of wild horses (and the
like), assume proportions under his hand truly
epic. *Mirèio, Vincen* (her lover), *Ourrias, Alari,*
are henceforth types to which the Arlesian
bard has set his seal. »

Athough the translator cannot hope that
his *version of Mirèio* will give the same degree
of pleasure as that derived from reading the
poet in his own language, still he hopes it
will give pleasure of the same kind, notwith-
standing any inferiority in strength and spirit
of his English to the Provençal.

---

1. On voit qu'il a sucé le lait d'une forte nature.

DEDICATION.

To Lamartine

To you I dedicate Mirèio :
'Tis my heart and soul;
It is the flower of my years;
It is a bunch of Crau grapes,
Which with all its leaves a peasant brings you.

Mistral.

Maillane (Bouches-du-Rhône), 8th September 1859.

MIRÈIO

CANTO I

THE FALABREGO-MAS [1]

A Provence [2] maid I sing,
Whom through the love-tale of her youth, the corn,
Across La Crau [3], far as the sea,
I mean to follow, as an humble pupil
Of great Homer. Being but a daughter
Of the soil she, beyond La Crau,
Was little known.

What though youth's halo only decked her brow!
What though she wore
No diadem of gold or damask cloak!
I'll have her raised to glory like a Queen,
And honored in our own despisèd tongue;
For 'tis for you we sing,
O shepherds and *mas*-dwelling folk.

Thou, Lord God of my country,
Who wast lowly among shepherds born,
With words of flame inspire me!
Thou knowest that amid the verdure,
In the sunshine, and at dew-fall,
When the figs are ripening, comes greedy
Wolfish man and quite despoils the tree.

But on the tree that he despoils
Some branch thou always raisest,
Tender, airy, which insatiate man
Cannot attain to ;
Odorous and virginal,
With Magdalen-ripe⁴ fruit, to which the birds
Will come their hunger to appease.

I see it now, the little branch:
Its freshness is provoking! yea, I see it
By the light breeze stirred and waving
In mid-air its foliage and immortal fruit.
Bright God! God friendly! help me on the wings
Of our Provençal tongue to reach
The branch aerial sacred to the birds!

Among the willows by the river-side,
·The Rhône with poplars bordered,
In a poor damp mouldy hut,
A basket-weaver dwelt,
Who, with his son
At times went round from *mas* to *mas,*
And patched old cribs and baskets full of holes.

One day as with their ozier-bundles shouldered
They were on their rounds,
Look at the sun! cries Vincen,
Father, look at Magalouno[5]!
How the clouds surround it!
If the rampart should come down,
We'll catch it, father, ere we reach the *mas*.

Oh! that's the *vent-larg*[6] rustling the leaves:
No, no, we shan't have rain,
The old man answered. Ah! if 'twere the Rau[7]
It would be different. Father, have they many
Ploughs at labor at the Falabrego?
Six, replied the basket-man.
Ah! that's the finest freehold in La Crau.

There, that's their olive-orchard!
Interspersed with rows of vine and almond-trees.
The beauty of it is,
(And there are not two like it on the coast,
The beauty of it is,) it has as many walks
As the whole year has days; and though there be
So many walks, in each there are as many trees.

Why, *caspitello*[8]! Vincen cried,
How many pickers they must need
To strip so many trees. Oh! that's all cared for:
Hallowmas is coming; the *Baussenco*[9] girls
Will quickly fill you sheets[10] and sacks
With olives green and purple. Many more
They'd gather, singing all the time.

While Master Ambroi talked
The sun behind the hills descended,
Tinting the light clouds with glowing hues.
The laborers were coming slowly
To their evening meal upon their yoked beasts
Sitting side-ways, with their goads erect.
The shades of night were low'ring on the distant moor.

I see their straw-heap on the treading-floor:
We're at the refuge, father;
Come along! cried Vincen.
But the old man noticed,
Here's the place for thriving sheep!
In summer they've the pine-wood, and in winter
The vast plain. They've, *hòu*[11]! plenty here.

And see the large trees there to shade the tiles;
And that delicious spring the vivary
Supplying; and the bees,
That every Autumn plunders,
Yet as soon as May ,awakes
The *falabrego*-trees encumber
With a hundred swarms.

Oh! then, in all the earth,
Here interrupted Vincen,
Father, what most charms me is
The *mas*-maid's self. If thou [12] remember, father,
She last summer ordered of us
Two new olive-picker's baskets, and moreover
Got us to put handles to her little hand one.

Talking on together thus
They reached the door.
The maid had just leaves given to her silkworms,
Now upon the door-step, in the dew,
Distaff in hand, she stood. Good evening
To the company! the basket-weaver,
Lowering his oziers, said.

The same to thee, returned the maid
To Master Ambroi.
I am threading this,
My distaff's point, you see. How late you are!
Where are you from? From Valabrego[13]?
Even so: it's late, we said, the Faiabrego
Are at hand; we'll sleep upon their straw-heap,

After which, without more words,
The weaver and his son
Upon a roller went and sat,
And set to work at once
Upon a cradle
Which already was begun,
And bent and crossed the supple ozier.

Certes, in face and figure
Vincen was a fine lad;
Hardly sixteen, cheeks
As swarthy as you choose;
But darkish land is known to yield
The finest wheat, and black grapes
Make the wine that sets all dancing.

How the ozier is prepared
And worked up, thoroughly he knew.
Not that on fine work
Usually he wrought; but mostly
Panniers made for beasts of burden,
And whatever needed was in farmsteads,
Such as rough, or neat and handy, baskets,

Split cane baskets,
Brooms of millet-grass, and many more
Such like; all ar.icles of ready sale.
He made them neatly, strong,
And quickly, with a master's hand.
But from the waste and fallow land
The laborers already had returned;

Already out of doors
The gentle maiden of the *mas*, Mirèio,
Had the platter set upon the table of stone;
Already were the servants of the farm
Their wooden ladles
Plunging into the capacious dish.
Meanwhile the old man and his son weaved on.

Then Master Ramoun, owner of the *mas*,
Ejaculated in his rather peevish tone,
How! Master Ambroi,
Not to supper coming?
Tut, man, put away the crib; the stars are out.
Mirèio, fetch a bowl.
Now come to supper for you must be tired.

Let's go, the basket-weaver said,
And to a corner of the table
They repaired and cut some bread.
Mirèio, graceful and alert,
With olive-oil seasoned them
A dish of beans,
And running brought it them.

Mirèio wasn't quite fifteen.
Blue coasts of Font-Vièio [14],
You Baussenco hills, and you Crau plains,
Have never since seen one so fair!
The cheery sun had hatched her!
And her fresh ingenuous face
A dimple on it had on either cheek.

Her look, as limpid as the dew-drop,
Banished sorrow;
Of the stars the rays
Less soft were and less pure;
Her bright black tresses fell about in wavy curls;
A double peach, not yet quite ripe,
Her rounded bosom seemed.

And somewhat shy;
Yet merry, laughter loving.
In a glass of water, ah! me,
Seeing so much beauty, you'd have drunk her up!
But to our tale. When every one,
As custom was, had spoken of his work,
As in my father's *mas* they used to, *I* ! *i* ! *i*! [15]

Has Master Ambroi got
No song to sing to us to-night?
They asked; it seems this is the meal to sleep at!
Peace, good friends, retorted the old man;
On him that jests God blows,
And makes him spin round like a top.
Lads, sing yourselves, you who are young and hearty.

Nay! but we're not jesting,
Master Ambroi, said the laborers;
But see! the Crau wine
In your goblet's running over:
Drink it off with us, good father.
Ah! rejoined the basket-weaver, in my youth
I was a singer; now, alas! my, lyre is broken. [16]

Master Ambroi, urged Mirèio,
Sing a song, please, 'twill enliven us.
The old man answered, Pretty maid,
There's nothing of my voice remaining but the husk;
If that can please you, it is ready.
Whereon, after emptying his goblet,
He began this song:

I

Bailly Suffren commanded at sea;
At Toulon he had hoisted his flag;
And we sailed in all five hundred brave Provençaux.
We were longing the English to thrash!
To our homes we would never return,
Till the Englishers utterly routed we'd seen.

II

But, behold, the first month of our cruize
From the shrouds we could nothing perceive
But the flying of hundreds and hundreds of gulls.
In the second month of our dull cruize
Certes a storm gave us trouble enough,
And we had to be baling out hard day and night.

III

In the third we were driven to madness,
Our blood boiled at finding no foe
For our thundering cannon to sweep from the sea.
Hands aloft! Suffren suddenly cries:
The main-top-man, then eagerly bent,
Spies away to the Arab coast on the lee-bow.

IV

When, *O tron de bon goi!* cries the man,
Three big vessels are bearing down on us!
Sharp, lads, run the guns to their ports, blaze away!
The great sailor immediately cried;
Let them first taste our figs of Antibes,
Ere we offer them some of a different sort.

V

But he hadn't yet said when one flash!
And like lightning forty large balls
Go to riddle the hulls of the Englishers' ships.
To one nothing was left but her soul!
Nought was heard but the roar of the guns,
And the cracking of wood, and the sea's dismal moans.

VI

From the foe now but one step divides us.
But one step ! what rapture ! what joy !
On the deck Bailly Suffren, intrepid and cool,
Stands erect, never wincing, and cries,
Cease your fire, lads, cease it and come,
Now's the time to anoint them well with Aix oil !

VII

But he hadn't yet said when the whole
Crew to hatchets, to cutlasses, rush,
And the bold Provençal with his grapnel in hand,
In one breath calls out, Board 'em, my boys !
At one spring to the Englisher's deck
We all jump, and 'twas then the great slaughter began.

VIII

Oh ! what blows ! oh ! what carnage ! what crashes
The mast falling makes on the deck !
And the deck broken in, and the men fighting still !
More than one of the Englishers falls
And expires ! More than one Provençal
In his arms takes the Englisher, strains him and dies !

It seems, eh ? quite incredible !
The good old father stopped him to observe.
It happened notwithstanding just as I have sung it.
Certes, we have a right to speak, for I
Was there myself the tiller holding. In my
Memory moreover, ha, ha ! should I live
A thousand years it would be stored up there.

What! you were at that awful slaughter?
Three to one they must have flattened you
As scythes are flat ened 'neath the beating hammer!
Who? the English? Cried the old tar,
Starting to his feet.
But presently the song he had begun
He, smiling proudly as before, resumed.

IX

With our feet in blood dabbling we fought on
From two postmeridian till night;
But, alas! when our eyes of the powder were free,
From our galley we missed five score men!
To the bottom however went three
Splendid ships of the king, England's king, with all han

X

Then upon our return to sweet home,
With a hundred shot-holes in our sides,
Yards in splinters, masts shivered, and sails all in rags,
The good Bailly thus friendly addressed us:
Go to, comrades, when I get there,
To the king of *Paris* I will speak of you all!

XI

O our admiral, free is your speech
We all answered; the king will hear you;
But for us, obscure mariners, what will he do?
All we had we had quitted, our homes
And our hamlets, to rush to his war
And defend him; and yet, you well know, we want bread

XII

But if yonder you do go, remember,
When all on your passage incline,
That none will e'er love you so well as your crew.
For believe us, good Suffren, we would,
Before seeking our homes, bear you king .
On the tips of our fingers ! had we but your leave.

XIII

'Twas a Martigau [17] made us this song,
While at vespers he spread out his nets.
Bailly Suffren departed for Paris forthwith.
They say that the great in those parts,
By his fame were to jealousy moved.
But his sailors beheld him no more, never more !

'Twas not too soon for the old man
To end his song,
His voice in tears was drowning ;
But the laborers enchanted were :
They sat with heads bent forward,
Mute, with lips apart, and for a while
E'en after it was over listened on.

And such like, said he,
Were the songs they sang when Martha span [18].
O youngsters, they were fine ;
Long-winded rather, and the tunes have got
A little old ; but what of that ? they sing
Now newer ones in French, in which the words
Are finer, but which no one understands.

At this remark of the old man
The laborers from table rose
And went to lead their six yoke to the stream,
And while their mules were drinking, they beneath
The branches pendent from the trellis
Still kept humming
The old Valabregan's song.

Mirèio loved a little talking,
And at table stayed
With Vincen, son to Master Ambroi.
Both together chatted,
And their heads would come together,
Part, and come together, like two
Cabridello [19] flowers in a merry wind.

Well, Vincen, says Mirèio,
When your bundle's on your shoulder,
And you go across the country mending baskets,
Don't you in your wanderings see,
Along with wild spots, haunted castles,
Lots of gorgeous palaces and brilliant *fêtes?*
Whereas we never leave our pigeon-house.

That's well said, my young lady.
Currants by their sharpness
Quench the thirst as well as drinking
From a jug; and if to get work
We must brave the weather,
Still the journey has its pleasures,
And the shady roadside compensates the heat.

Accordingly as soon as summer comes,
And all the olive-trees
Are draped with flowers,
On the ash-trees in the whitened orchards,
Guided by the scent,
We go and hunt the cantharis
Green glistening in the heat of day.

These the shops buy of us.
Sometimes upon the *garrigo* [20]
We pick the red oak-apple : sometimes
In the ponds we go and fish blood-suckers.
O brave sport ! no need of net or bait !
You've only got to beat the water
And the leech comes sticking to your legs !

But thou wast never at Li Santo [21] ?
Dear soul, that's the place for singing !
There it is that from all parts the sick are brought.
We passed it on the *fête*-day.
Of a truth the church is small.
Nevertheless, what offerings and vows !
Such cries ! Great Saints ! great Saints ! have pity on us.

Twas the year of the great miracle.
Moun Diéu ! what a sight !
A sickly child was on the pavement weeping,
Pretty as St John the Baptist !
Presently he raised a sad and plaintive voice,
O Saints ! O Saints ! restore my sight !
I'll bring you my pet lambkin with the budding horns.

All round him were in tears.
The reliquaries meanwhile lighted
Slowly from above upon the prostrate people;
And no sooner had the cable [22]
Slacked a little when the whole church,
Like a strong wind in the forest,
Cried, O great Saints, come! oh! come and save us!

In the arms of his godmother now,
The child put forth his little slender fingers,
And the reliquaries clutched,
Which held the bones
Of the three blessed Marys,
With the desperation of the drowning man
To whom the sea has heaved a plank.

The child no sooner had
The Saints' bones seized (I saw it!)
Than he cried, with faith
Most marvellous, I see
The wonder-working reliquaries! and I see
Grandmother all in tears! Come, let's go quick
And fetch my lambkin with the budding horns.

As for thyself, young lady, God preserve thee
Happy, handsome! But should ever dog
Or lizard, wolf or snake, or any other
Prowling, creeping, creature,
Wound thee with its fang;
Should e'er misfortune overtake thee,
Hie thee to the Saints, thou'lt surely get relief.

So sped the evening.
The unharnessed large-wheeled cart
No lengthy shadow cast.
From time to time a bell was heard
To tinkle in the marshes,
And the dreamy owl sad lamentations
Added to the nightingale's sweet song.

As on the mere and trees to-night
The moon is shining,
Vincen pleaded, wilt thou
Let me tell thee of a race
In which I thought to win the prize?
I will, replied the maiden ; and with bated breath
The simple child approached him more than happy.

'Twas at Nismes, Mirèio,
Ou the Esplanade, that these foot-races
Were in vogue. At Nismes there was a crowd
Collected thicker than a shock of hair
To see the sport.
Already many runners were prepared
To run ; all hatless, coatless, shoeless ;

When the king of runners, Lagalanto,
All at once appears !
Who of Provence and eke of Italy
The swiftest had outstripped.
The mighty Lagalanto !
Lagalanto, the renowned Marseilles man !
Sure his name's familiar to thine ears.

Equal to the Seneschal John of Cossa's [23]
He had legs! yea, he had thighs!
And too of pewter-plates he had a dresser full,
On which his races were engraved;
Besides, so many splendid scarfs had he, Mirèio,
That against the wainscot thou hadst sworn
The rainbow stood expanded!

Seeing him, the other runners
Hurried on their clothes again.
No one with Lagalanto dared to run.
Lou Cri, a lad of training,
And who had not flaccid legs,
Had come to Nismes that day with cows.
Alone he dared to challenge him.

Name of a rat! cried I,
(I, who was only there by chance;)
But we too are a runner!
Oh! what had I said, fool that I was!
They all surround me! You must run!
Now judge. I'd never run but after partridges:
Then only with the oaks for witnesses.

But I was forced to.
Lagalanto, when he saw me,
Took me up with, Fasten your shoe-latchets [24],
My poor boy! The muscles meanwhile
Of his own stout limbs he was encasing
In silk-hose, to which were tacked
Ten little golden bells.

Our breath to garner, each
A bit of willow put into his mouth.
In haste and friendly we shake hands.
Then, trembling with impatience
And excitement, each, with one foot
On the line, awaits the signal.
It is given! Like a lightning-flash we

Scour the plain!
We tear along; it's you! it's I!
A cloud of dust impedes our springs;
Our hair smokes!
Ah! what ardor! what a mad race!
Long all thought abreast we'd reach the goal;
Such was the spirit that impelled us!

Finally I take the lead!
But this was truly my misfortune;
For, the instant, like a fool,
I forward sprang   .
And passed them,
Down I fell, pale and expiring,
Rolled and bit the dust!

The other two continued running,
Steady, ever steady,
Like the *chivau-frus* [25] at Aix.
The famous Marseillais thought *him*-self
Sure of winning. It was said he had no spleen!
The Marseillais, young lady, notwithstanding
Found his man in Lou Cri of Mouriès [26].

Now they the throng of spectators had passed,
And had already nearly reached the goal.
O beauty mine, hadst thou but seen him, Lou Cri, sprin
Neither on mountains nor in parks was ever
Stag or hare with so much nerve
For running seen! Him after Lagalanto
Rushes, howling like a wolf!

Lou Cri with glory's crowned.
He hugs the winning post for joy!
All Nismes comes flocking up
His birthplace to enquire.
The plate of pewter blazes in the sun!
The hautboys flourish and the cymbals clang!
Lou Cri receives the pewter-plate.

And Lagalanto? asks Mirèio.
Sitting on the ground, enveloped
In the dust the people raised about him,
Clasping both his knees,
His soul stung with th'affront that so defiled him,
He shed bitter tears that mingled
With the drops that from his forehead fell.

Lou Cri approaches and salutes him.
Brother, says he, come! let's to the arbour
Of the inn repair, behind the large *areno* 27
Yonder, and the money-over 28 drink:
To-morrow's time enough for wailing;
Pleasure rules to-day! for thee,
As well as me, go to, there's sun enough left still.

Then Lagalanto, tearing
From his trembling limbs
The hose with golden bells,
His pallid visage raised and said,
Since age undoes me, there, they're thine!
Thou, Cri, whom youth decks like a swan,
May'st honorably wear the strong man's gear.

These were his words.
And in the dense crowd,
Mournful as an ash bereft of head,
The whilom king of runners disappeared.
Nor on St John's day, nor St Peter's,
Never since has he been seen to run,
Or jump upon th' inflated hide [29].

Thus Vincen did expatiate on things
He knew, before the Falabrego-Mas;
His cheeks waxed crimson,
And his dark eyes flashed;
Whate'er he uttered he gesticulated,
And his speech abounded like a sudden
Heavy may-shower on a mown-grass field.

The crickets chirruping among the clods
Ceased more than once to listen;
Oft the night-bird, oft the nightingale,
Kept silent; she too
Sitting on the leafy branch-heap,
To the bottom of her soul impressed,
Till early dawn would not have closed an eye.

'Tis my opinion that he,
For a basket weaver's son,
Speaks wonderfully well, she to her mother said.
O mother! it is sweet to sleep in winter.
Now the nights are light, too light to sleep:
Let's listen, listen to him! I would pass
My vigils and my life in hearing him!

NOTES

TO THE FIRST CANTO

——

1. — The word *mas*, meaning a countryhouse, farm or homestead, is especially used in the *arrondissement* of Arles, and in Languedoc. In eastern Provence the word *bastido* is used in preference, and in the *comtat* that of *granjo*. To every *mas* a name is attached which distinguishes and characterises it, as the *Mas de la Font*, the *Mas de l'Osle*, the *Mas Crema*, the *Mas di Falabrego*. The *falabrego* is the fruit of a sort of lotus, called in French *micocoulier*, and in Provençal *falabreguié*, the *cellis australis* of Linnæus; it is a large tree, common in Provence. The words *mas* and *falabrego* are both of Celtic origin. It is even held that Marseilles, *Massalia*, comes from *Mas Salyum*, habitation of the Salii.

2. — *Provence*, formerly one of the provinces of France, comprises the departments of the Bouches-du Rhône, the Var, the Lower-Alps, and portions of Vaucluse and the Drôme. Previous to the union it had been governed successively by eighteen Counts, of whom René, *ex-king* of Naples, styled *le bon Roi René*, Charles, 3rd

Count of Maine, and Louis XI, king of France, were the last. It was united to the French crown by Charles VIII in 1487. The climate of Provence is beautiful and healthy Its soil is very fertile in many parts, but perfeetly. sterile in others. Its principal rivers are the Rhône, the Durance, the Argens, the Var, the Verdon and the Sorgues. The language of Provence was one of the first cultivated in the middle ages; it is remarkable for its rhythm and softness. The poets of Provence were the Troubadours, so called from *troubar* to find or invent; of whom the most celebrated were Pierre Vidal, Arnauld Daniel, Bertrand de Born, Bernard de Ventadour, Faydit Raymond Béranger (Count of Provence), Richard I, *cœur de lion* (King of England), and William IX, Count of Poitiers. — *Translator.*

3. — *La Crau* (from the Greek xραῦρος, arid), is a vast arid stony plain, bounded on the North by the *Alpines* (Lower Alps), on the East by the meres of Martigue, on the West by the Rhône, and on the South by the sea. It is the Arabia Petrea of France, and is, by the canal of Craponne, traversed and interspersed with oases.

4. — *Magdalen-ripe fruit*, that which ripens about St Magdalen's day, the 22d of July. — T.

5. — *Magalouno* is situated on the sea-marge of the Hérault. Of this city, originally a Greek colony, nothing now remains but a church in ruins. Mr Moquin Tandon, a member of the *Institut* and a Languedocian poet, has written a work entitled *Carya Magalonensis*, in *langue romane*, containing an interesting chronicle of the principal events of which this town was the theatre in the beginning of the 14th century.

6. — *Vent-larg*, sea breeze.

7. — *The Rau*, westerly wind.

8. — *Caspitello*, or *càspi*, an interjection corresponding to *dame! tudieu !*

9. — *The Baussenco girls.* Li Baus, in French *les Baux* is a town in ruins, formerly the capital of the princely house of Baux. « Three leagues from Arles, on the rocky summit of one of the Alpines, are scattered the ruins of a town which, from the grandeur of its site, the antiquity of its foundation, and the important place it holds in the annals of the country, allures the traveller, kindles the imagination of the artist, offers to the curiosity of the archœologist abundant matter, and irritates and often confounds his learned sagacity. » (Jules Canonge's history of the town of Les Baux in Provence.)

As the name of this poetical locality ofter occurs in the poem, we think the reader will be pleased with the following description of it by the same author.

« At length there opened out before me a narrow valley. I bowed to the remains of a stone cross that sanctify the way, and when I raised my eyes they were riveted with astonishment on a set of towers and walls on the top of a rock the like of which I had never before seen, save in works in which the genius of painting had been inspired by the most fabulous imaginings of Ariosto. But if my surprise was great at the first aspect, it was doubly so when I had reached an eminence whence the whole town was displayed to view. It was a spectacle of desolate grandeur, such as a perusal of the Prophets presents to the mind; it was something I had never suspected the existence of, a town almost monolothite. Those who first had the idea of inhabiting the rock, had hewed them a shelter out of its sides. This novel mode of architecture was plainly approved of by their successors, for soon from the vast compact mass a town issued, like a statue from a block touched by the wand of art. An imposing town with its fortifications, chapels and hospitals; a town in which man seemed to have eternalised his habitation. The dominion of the city was extensive, and brilliant feats of arms have secured for it a noble place in history; but it has proved no more enduring than so many others less solidly constructed. ›

The action of the poem begins at the foot of these ruins.

10. — *Sheets* spread to catch the olives as they are shaken from the trees. — T.

11. — *Hòu.* The vowels of this exclamation are pronounced separately, the *ò* as in English, and the *u* as in *ou* or *où* in French. — The *é* in *Diéu* (a word often recurring in the poem), is sounded as *é* in French, and the *u* as in *hòu*; but in both words the tone is louder on the penultimate vowel. — T.

12. — *If thou remember, father.* *Vous* in Provençal, as in French, is the pronoun of respect, deference, ceremony and reverence, and corresponds to *thou*, *thee*. — T.

13. — *Valabrego*, a village situate on the left bank of the Rhône, between Avignon and Tarascon.

14. — *Font-Vièio*, a village in one of the valleys of the Alpines in the neighbourhood of Arles.

15. — *I! i! i!* written *Ai! ai! ai!* a Provençal interjection corresponding to *oh! ah! alas!* and pronounced precisely as our vowel *i* is — T.

16. — *My lyre is broken.*

« The shrill cigala strikes his lyre. »

B^p HEBER. — T.

The Provençal word *mirau* means the two membranes shining and sonorous that the cigala has under the abdomen, and which by concussion produce the sound known in France by *chant*. It is proverbially said of a person whose voice has been impaired by age, *a li mirau creba*.

17. — *A Martigau*, an inhabitant of Martigue, a curious town of Provence, inhabited almost exclusively by fishermen, built on some small islands, intersected by the salt lakes and narrow channels of the sea by way of streets, which has occasioned it to be surnamed *la Venise provençale*. It was the birth place of Gérard Tenque, (*Thom* or *Tung*, — T.) the founder of the order of St John of Jerusalem.

18. — *When Martha span*, a proverbial expression signifying, *in more happy times, in the good old days*, in allusion probably to Martha, Christ's hostess, who, after having according to the legend delivered Tarascon of the monster that ravaged its territory, ended her days in those parts. She inhabited a small house on the banks of the Rhône, at the door of which she would sit, surrounded by her neophytes, modestly plying her spinning wheel.

19. — *Cabridello*, a plant common in the marshes of the South, the *aster tripolium*, Lin.

20· — *The garrigo*, li garrigo, barren lands where nothing but the dwarf-oak, the *agarrus*, grows.

21. — *Li Santo*, is the Provençal name of a small town of 543 inhabitants, situate in the isle of Camargue on

the seashore between the mouths of the Rhône. In obe-
dience to a poetical and venerable tradition, an innume-
rable host of pilgrims from every part of Provence and
lower Languedoc assemble at this place every 25th of
May. The tradition is as follows :

After the death of Christ, the Jews constrained some of
the most fervent disciples to enter a dismantled ship, and
consigned them to the mercy of the waves. The scene
is thus described in an old French canticle.

LES JUIFS.

Entrez, Sara, dans la nacelle,
Lazare, Marthe et Maximin,
Cléon, Trophime, Saturnin,
Les trois Maries et Marcelle,
Eutrope et Martial, Sidoine avec Joseph (d'Arimathie),
Vous- périrez dans cette nef.

Allez, sans voile et sans cordage,
Sans mât, sans ancre, sans timon,
Sans aliments, sans aviron,
Allez faire un triste naufrage !
Retirez-vous d'ici, laissez-nous en repos,
Allez crever parmi les flots !

Guided by Providence, the bark gently stranded on the
extremity of the isle of Camargue in Provence. The poor
exiled believers having miraculously escaped the perils
of the sea, dispersed over southern Gaul and became
its first apostles.

Mary Magdalen, one of the three Marys, retired to the
desert of La Ste Baume to weep over her sins. The
two others, Mary the mother of St James the less,
and Mary of Salome, the mother of the two apostles,
St John the Evangelist and St James the Great, accom-
panied by their maid Sarah, after converting to the new

faith some of the neighbouring people, returned to the place of their landing to die (see xi canto).

Mr B. Laurens, who has described and sketched in l'*Illustration* (vol. xx, p. 7) the pilgrimage of the St Marys, adds, « It is reported that a prince, whose name is not mentioned, knowing that the bodies of the St Marys were interred at this spot, built a church over it in the form of a citadel, so that it might be safe from piratical invasion. He also built houses round the church, and ramparts for the safety of the inhabitants. The buildings that remain bear out the tradition perfectly well.

» In 1448, after hearing a sermon on the blessing Provence enjoyed in possessing the remains of the St Marys, king René visited the church built in their honor, caused a search to be made for the holy bones, and the success of his undertaking was revealed by the marvellous odor that arose as the body of each (saint) was discovered. It is needless to tell of all the honor paid to, and all the care taken of, these relics. »

22. — *No sooner had the cable slacked.* « The choir of the church presents the peculiarity of being composed of three stories : a crypt, which is pointed out as being the very spot of the ancient oratory of the Saints ; a sanctuary raised higher than usual ; and a chapel above, where the reliquaries are exposed. Innumerable tapers are held lighted by the congregation, and on the capstern being unwound, the chain of which is attached to the reliquary, the latter slowy descends from the chapel above into the choir. This is the moment propitious to miracles. When also immense supplication arises on all sides ; St Marys, heal my child ! or such like is the piercing cry raised, drawing tears from the coldest heart. All await, singing canticles the while, till the

moment comes to get a poor blind or epileptic man to sit upon the reliquary, and when this is achieved all believe themselves heard. » (B. Laurens.)

23. *John of Cossa*, a Neapolitan noble who had followed King René; he was grand seneschal of Provence and died in 1476. John of Cossa is very popular at Tarascon, where the people ascribe to him the building of St Martha's steeple. He is interred in the crypt of that church, and his statue in a recumbent attitude surmounts the tomb.

24. — *Fasten your shae-latchets*, a proverbial expression signifying, *prepare for a sharp run.*

25. — *The chivau-frus*; these are painted cardboard horses, used in Provence at public rejoicings, and particularly at Aix at the *Fête-Dieu.* The seeming riders attach them to their waists, and prancing parade the streets to the sound of the tambourin.

26. — *Mouriès*, a village south of the Alpines.

27. — *The large Areno*, the Roman amphitheatre at Nismes. — T.

28. — *The money over*, (lis estreno,) the money collected for the *fête* remaining over after the expenses have been all paid. — T.

29. — *The inflated hide*, usually a sheep or goat skin, on which the performer stands, jumps, or dances. — T.

MIRÈIO

CANTO II

THE LEAF-PICKING

Sing away, sing away, *magnanarello* [1] !
Leaf-picking disposes to singing;
The silkworms are fine and are sleeping their third [2]
The mulberry-trees too are full of young maids,
Whom the beautiful weather enlivens;
They look like a swarm of brown bees in a field,
From the rosemary filching the honey.

Sing away, sing away, *magnanarello!*
While stripping your boughs, sing away!
Mirèio was picking one lovely May morn;
For earrings, that very May morning,
To her ears the coquette
Had fastened two cherries.
It happened that Vincen was passing that way.

In his bright-scarlet cap,
As the Latin sea-shore people wear,
He had jauntily set a cock's feather.
While footing the paths
The stray adders he routed,
And from the stone-heaps
With his stick he sent flying the flints.

Ho! Vincen! Mirèio called out
From the midst of the straight verdant walks,
You are passing full fast, why so?
Vincen directly the alley returned to,
Detected the maid on a mulberry-tree perched
Like a grey-crested lark [3],
And delighted flew to her.

The leaf, Mirèio, comes off briskly;
Little by little and all will be picked.
May I help thee? You may. While above
She was laughing for joy,
Vincen sprang from the clover
And climbed up the tree like a squirrel.
Old Master Ramoun hath but thee, Mirèio;

Better do the lower branches,
I'll the top ones manage.
With her light hand stripping off the leaves,
She said, It keeps off melancholy thoughts
To work in company: alone,
A sort of dreariness comes over one.
Ah! so there does, returned the youth;

For when we're yonder in our hut
And only hear the impetuous Rhône
Over the shingle rushing,
Oh! how dreary 'tis sometimes!
Not so much so in summer, for
Father and I then on our errands go
From one *mas* to the other;

But no sooner has the holly reddened
And the winter set in, when the nights are long,
And round the hearth half out
There whistles at the latch, or mews,
Some goblin; and with little talking
And less light I must till bed time come
Sit up alone with him....

Here giddily the maiden interrupted,
But your mother, where is she? She's dead.
The lad was for a moment silent.
Then pursued: When Vinceneto
Was along with us and, though quite young,
Still kept the hut, there was some pleasure.
But what *are* you saying, Vincen?

You've a sister? And the lass is good
And clever too, the ozier-bender added;
For at Font-dou-Rèi yonder, in the land
Of Beaucaire, whither she had gone, the reapers
Following, her grace and skill attracted notice
So much that as servant she was taken
And has been there ever since.

Are you considered like your little sister?
Who, I? not a bit! she's fair
And I am brown, thou seest, as a berry.
Knowest thou of whom she does remind me?
Yea, of thee! your two bright heads,
With hair. abounding like the myrtle's foliage,
Might for twins be taken.

But the knack of tightening
The light muslin of thy cap[4], Mirèio,
Better far than she thou hast.
My sister's neither plain nor dull,
But how much handsomer art thou!
Mirèio here let slip her half culled branch
And cried, Oh! what a Vincen!

Sing away, sing away, *magnanarello!*
For fine are the leaves of the mulberry-trees;
The silkworms are fine and are sleeping their third;
The mulberry-trees too are full of young maids
Whom the beautiful weather enlivens:
They look like a swarm of brown bees in a field
From the rosemary filching the honey.

Then you find me pretty?
More so than your sister?
Much more! answered he
And what more have I, pray?
Mother divine! What has the goldfinch
More than the frail wren? an't be not
Beauty melody and grace!

What more! O my poor sister,
You'll not get the white out of the leek!
Why, Vinceneto's eyes are like sea-water,
Blue and limpid; thine are black as jet;
And when on me they shine,
Methinks I'm draining off
A bumper of cooked wine [5].

When she would sing the *Peirounello*,
In her silvery clear voice,
I loved to listen to my sister's melody.
But, O young lady, every little word
Thou sayest to me far more charms
My ear, disturbs my heart,
Than could a thousand melodies.

With running in the pastures
In the sun, my sister's face and neck
All browne l are like a bunch of dates;
Whereas thou, beauty, I believe art fashioned
Like the flowers of the asphodel,
And that thy fair brow with his tawny hand
Summer dares not caress.

My sister's slender as the dragonfly
That skims the rivulet:
Poor little one! she grew up in one year.
But from the shoulder to the hip,
In thee, Mirèio, nothing is amiss!
Again she, letting slip her branch and blushing
Crimson, cries, Oh! what a Vincen!

Sing away, sing away, *magnanarello !*
While stripping your boughs.
The two well-favored children,
Hidden by the leafy branches,
In the innocency of their age
Were learning to make love.
Meanwhile the clouds were clearing off the hills,

And there were seen
Over the large ruined towers, whither
Nightly the old Lords of Baux return,
And high above the bare rocks,
Vultures [6] with their large white wings refulgent
Soaring to the sun
Already warm.

Oh, we've done nothing ! what a shame !
Cried she as if vexed.
See now, *some* one said he'd come to help me
Then this some one nothing does but talk
And make me laugh. Redeem your promise; otherwis
She'll say, my mother, truly I'm unfit,
Yea, far too awkward, to be married yet.

Alas ! my boasting friend,
I think if you for wages were engaged
To pick leaves by the quintal,
And the sprigs were handed to you,
You'd e'en then eat *regardello* [7] !
Thou then for a gawky takest me !
The lad not slightly crest-fallen cries.

We'll see, young lady,
Who'll the better picker prove !
And bravely with both hands they set to work
To bend and strip the branches.
No more resting, no more idle talking :
(Sheep that baas her mouthful loses :)
Presently the mulberry-tree is stripped.

The leaves must now
Be put into a sack.
Oh ! what a fine thing youth is !
Once the pretty taper fingers
Of the damsel in the *arescle* 8
Entangled got with the brown burning fingers
Of that Vincen.

She and he both started ! flushed with love.
Both felt the flame as of some fire unknown.
Then as she with affright
Her hands was taking from the leaves,
The lad still quivering with emotion said,
What is the matter with thee ?
Has a hidden hornet

Peradventure stung thee ?
In an undertone with lowered head,
I don't know, she replied.
Again they both began without more speech
To pick a few sprigs; but with roguish
Downcast eyes they one another watched
To see who'd laugh the first.

Their hearts beat fast.
Once more the leaves were showered down;
And when the time for sacking came again,
The white hand and the brown hand,
Whether purposely or haply,
Always met! The work went on
And was enjoyed all the same.

Sing away, sing away, *magnanarello!*
While stripping your branches.
See! see! all at once Mirèio cries;
See! what's that? While she briskly, as a lark
Upon a vine, put one forefinger to her lips
And with the other pointed to a bird's nest
Opposite the branch herself was perched on.

Wait a bit! With bated breath
And like a sparrow
Vincen hops from branch to branch
Towards the bird's nest.
At the bottom of a hole that had been
Naturally formed within the bark
The little ones were visible, all fledged and lively.

Vincen who had straddled
With his vigorous legs the crooked bough,
By one hand holding on feels with the other
In the hollow trunk. A little higher up
Mirèio sat with glowing cheeks.
What sort? She softly asks.
Rare beauties! What of? Blue tomtits!

Mirèio burst out lauging.
Listen, said she; did you never hear
That when two find a nest
Upon a mulberry-tree or any other,
Holy church will join you
Ere twelve months pass?
And proverbs, father says, are always trusty.

Yes, returned he, but remember
That this hope may vanish
If the little ones escape before they're caged.
Ieuse, moun Diéu! cries the maiden,
Put them safely by at once,
For it concerns us!
Faith, the safest place to put them by in,

Answered the young man,
Methinks would be thy bodice.
Ah! of course. Whereon the lad
Dips one hand down into the hollow,
And his hand returning full
Exhibits four tomtits. *Bondiéu!*
Shouts Mirèio, both hands raising.

Oh! how many! what a pretty brood!
There, there, poor little ones, one kiss!
And wild with pleasure with a thousand kisses
She devours and coaxes them;
Then lovingly and softly
Puts them by within her bodice.
There, hold out thy hand again! cries Vincen.

Oh ! the beauties, she continues;
In their blue heads they have little eyes
As sharp as needles. Then within the smooth
White prison she bestows three more;
And into the warm bosom of the maiden
Nestling down, the wee brood fancies itself
To the bottom of its nest restored.

But Vincen, seriously, are there any more?
Yes. Holy Virgin ! then I do declare
A charmed hand you must have.
Eh ! simple maiden, tomtits will about St George's
Lay you ten twelve eggs, and e'en fourteen,
Many a time. But here, take these,
The last hatched. And now *good* by, pretty hollow !

Hardly had the youth said,
Scarce had she arranged the brood
And in her flowered neckerchief
Enveloped it,
When, *I ! i ! i !* the poor girl cries,
And modestly upon her bosom
Pressing both hands, *I ! i ! i !* I'm dying !

Houi ! houi ! weeping now, they're scratching me,
They scratch ! *I ! i !* and sting ! O Vincen run up quick
The fact is that just then,
What shall I say? a great commotion reigned
And lively in the hiding place
Among the fledglings; those last hatched
Had brought confusion with them ;

And within the narrow vale
The sportive brood
To settle freely down unable,
Scrambled up and down with claw and wing,
And o'er the undulating hills and down
The sloping mounds a thousand somersets
And pretty rolls performed.

I ! i! come take them quickly,
Murmurs she : and like a vine-branch
Trembling in the wind, or like a heifer
Stung with cattle-flies ;
So moans, writhes, bends,
The maiden of the Falabrego-Mas.
He climbs to reach the branch she's on.

Sing away, sing away, *magnanarello !*
While stripping your boughs :
To the branch she is weeping on now he has got.
The tickling thou dislikest
Greatly then ? he kindly asked.
Ah ! if like me through nettles barefoot
Thou hadst oft to go,

What wouldst thou do ? I wonder !
Then he offers cheerily his sea-cap
To transfer the birdies to.
Mirèio quickly slips her hand
Beneath the neckerchief,
And one by one the cap receives
The little beauties of tomtits.

But now her eyes are lowered
And her face averted is a little,
Poor dear! Soon however smiles
Return and stay her tears; e'en like
The dew that in the early morning,
Wets the flowers and grass,
Then rolls up into little pearls and passes off.

Now suddenly the branch
They both were on
Snaps and assunder breaks!
She shrieking, to the ozier-bender's neck springs
And around it throws her arms:
Then from the large tree with a rapid twirl
Both fall, together folded, on the supple rye-grass!

O ye zephyrs, *Larg* and *Gregoli* [10],
The wood's green canopy cease shaking!
O'er the young pair hush your merry whispers!
Silence for one moment.
Foolish breezes, softly breathe!
Give them a little time to dream!
The time at least to dream of happiness!

Thou that art prattling in thy bed,
Hush! gently, little stream!
Over thy sounding pebbles make less noise!
Not so much noise!
For their two souls have to the same
Bright region sped. Leave them to wander
In their starry sky!

A moment after, from the close embrace
She disengaged herself.
The blossoms of the quince-tree
Never were so pale! Then on the bank
They sit; awhile on one-another gaze;
And this is how in dudgeon spoke
The lad of oziers.

Shame, oh! shame of trees!
The devil's tree! a Friday planted tree!
Let the blight seize thee!
And the woodlouse eat thee! May thy master
Ever more in horror hold thee!
Say, art thou not hurt, Mirèio?
Trembling with emotion she replied.

No, I'm not hurt, oh! no.
But like a swaddled child, oft crying
Without knowing why, I have here something
That disturbs me; it prevents my hearing,
Blinds me, makes my heart boil, and my brain
Is ever full of it; my blood
My body courses through and won't keep quiet.

May be 'tis, the basket-weaver said,
The fear thy mother will for having been
Too long about the picking scold thee?
Like me when I came in out of hours
From a blackberry-excursion,
Tattered, blackened like a Moor.
Oh! no, Mirèio said, another sort of pain

It is. Or possibly a sun-stroke
May have dazed thee, Vincen urged;
I know upon the Baux hills an old woman,
One named Taven, who a glass of water
Sets upon your forehead, when the charmed rays
Swiftly from the dazed brain
Pass into the crystal.

No, oh! no, replied the Crau maid;
Floods of May sun never yet were known
'To fright Crau maidens.
But why keep you longer in suspense?
My bosom cannot hold it! Will you know it,
Vincen? Vincen, you I love!
The hoary close-pruned willows,

River's banks, the green grass
And the ambient air,
Were fairly wrapped in glee!
Alas! princess, that thou so fair,
Replied the basket-weaver's son,
Shouldst have a tongue so wicked!
'Tis enough to stupify and dumbfound!

What now! thou in love with me?
Mirèio, don't of my poor life
Still happy go and make a jest;
Don't try and make me credit things
Which here once stored might afterwards
My death occasion. No, Mirèio,
Never more in this sort langh at me.

May God me ne'er *imparadise*
If in my words a lie there be !
Go to, believe I love you; that won't kill you, Vincen!
But if out of cruelty
You will not have me for your lover,
'Twill be me then, sick with sorrow,
'Twill be me you'll see consuming at your feet.

Oh! say no more such things.
'Tween thee and me there is a labyrinth,
Said desp'rately the son of Master Ambroi.
Of the Falabrego-Mas thou art
The Queen, to whom all bow, Mirèio;
Whilst I'm *but* a vagrant
Valabregan basket-weaver.

Eh ! and what care I, returned she,
Sharp and fiery as a *ligarello* [11],
An my lover be a Baron
Or a basket-maker, so he please me?
But and if you care not to have languor
Drink my blood, why even in your tatters,
Vincen, do you look so handsome?

Facing the enchanting virgin,
Dizzy as a slowly-falling
Fascinated bird [12] he felt.
Thou must be then a witch, pursued he,
For the sight of thee to daunt me thus,
Thy voice to mount into my head and make me
Foolish as a man o'ercome with drink !

Seest *thou* not thy embrace
Has set my brain on fIre?
For lo, if thou must know it, even
At the risk that thou of me a poor
Pack-bearer wilt but make thy laughingstock,
I'll tell thee that I love thee too, Mirèio;
Love thee e'en with so much love I could devour thee

Love thee so, that if thy lips should say
I want the golden goat [13], the goat no mortal
Tends nor milks, which 'neath
Baus-maniero [14] rock licks off the moss;
I should or perish in the quarries,
Or produce the goat with golden [15] hair,
As thou shouldst see!

I love thee, O enchanting maid, so much,
That shouldst thou say I want a star!
There is no sea to cross nor torrent wild,
There is no headsman fire nor steel,
That should arrest me: to the peak's top
Even to the sky I'd go and take the star,
And Sunday thou shouldst have it to thy neck.

O passing beautiful! the more I gaze on thee
The more I'm dazzled.
In my path I saw a fig-tree [16] once
Out of the bare rock growing,
Near the grotto of Vaucluse;
So spare, alas! that to the lizards grey
A sprig of jasmine had more shade afforded:

Round about its roots, once every year,
The neighbouring stream comes gushing,
And the arid shrub of the abundant water
Rising to refresh it drinks its fill;
And this one drink the whole year round suffices it.
E'en as the stone is cut to fit the ring,
To us this parable applies.

For I, Mirèio, am the fig-tree;
Thou the fountain and its freshness art.
It would for me suffice if once a year
I might on bended knees as now
Myself sun in the beams of thy sweet countenance
Above all if I might but touch
With trembling lips thy fingers!

Palpitating with young love, Mirèio
Listened. Then he takes her,
He bewildered folds her in his arms!
He her bewildered presses; when, Mirèio!
In the avenue resounds
The voice of an old woman; and the silkworms!
What are they to have to eat at noon?

A flight of sparrows
Lighting in high spirits on a pine-tree
Will with cheery chirping
Fill the evening air;
But if the gleaner watching them
A stone flings suddenly, on all sides
They affrighted fly off to the wood.

Thus in a tremor of emotion
Fled across the fields
Th' enamoured pair. She to the *mas*
Without a word proceeds, her leaves upon her head
He stopping soon, stands, as if spell-bound,
Gazing at her running
O'er the fallow until lost to sight.

NOTES

TO THE SECOND CANTO

———

1. — *Magnanarello* are women silkworm—rearers. *Magnan* are silkworms.

2. — *Sleeping their third.* Silkworms live in the larva-state thirty-four days about, and in this interval moult, or shed their skin, four times. At the approach of each of these periods they become as it were paralysed and cease eating, *dormon.* They say in Provençal, *dourmi de la proumiero, di dos, di tres, di quatre,* which means literally, sleeping the first, second, third, fourth (moult).

3. — *A grey-crested lark,* the *alauda cristata,* Lin.

4. — *The light muslin of thy cap.* The Crau women wear their hair tightly enveloped in a kerchief of fine transparent linen or muslin, around which is passed a band of velvet, usually of a blue black, at a distance of about one-third from the top of the muslin, leaving therefore so much of it visible; another turn is then passed immediately below the first, and then another, until the

two-thirds of the muslin are concealed. The black band
is finally fastened at the back of the head with a large
gold pin, while the end, to the length of about a foot, is
left pendent. On either side of the forehead the hair is
suffered to fall as low as the cheek-bone, where it is
gracefully curved back and gathered under the muslin.
— T.

5. - *Cooked wine.* The grape-juice on being removed
from the press is boiled in a cauldron, and after one year's
bottle has the color and flavor of the best Spanish wines.
The Provençaux drink it at feasts, galas, and always at
Christmas.

6. — *Vultures,* the *vultur percnoptus,* Gm.

7. — *Regardello* are imaginary dishes. *Manja de regar-
dello* means eating with the eyes, or *mâcher à vide,* as
Rabelais expresses it.

8. — *Arescle* is a hoop adapted to the mouth of a sack
to keep it open. The name of *arescle* is generally given
to the wood used in making drums, strainers, sieves,
bushels, etc.

9. — *Margai* is the *lolium perenne* of Linnœus, or the
ray or rye-grass of the English.

10. — *Gregali, gregau,* or *grè,* are words used to
signify the Greek, or N. E. wind.

11. — *Ligarello,* a female sheaf-binder.

12. — *A fascinated bird* (*auceu pivela*). The verb
pivela or *pipa* indicates the action, real or imaginary, by

which a reptile attracts to itself a bird, and even a person. The people ascribe this attraction to some irresistible inspiration, which nevertheless may be intercepted by the sudden passage of any foreign body.

13. — *The golden goat (la cabro d'or)*, is a phrase used to signify some treasure or talisman that the people imagine has been buried by the Saracens under one or other of the antique monuments of Provence. Some allege that it lies under the mausoleum of St Remy, others under the Baux rocks.

« This tradition » says George Sand (in *Les visions de la nuit dans les campagnes,*) « is universal; there are few ruins, castles or monasteries, few celtic monuments, that have not their own treasure hidden away some where, all guarded by some diabolic animal. Mr Jules Canonge, in a charming collection of southern tales, has rendered graceful and beneficent the poetical apparition of *the golden goat*, the guardian of the riches hidden in the bosom of the earth. »

The tradition of a treasure that assumes innumerable forms, but all having their *raison d'être*, and guarded by some strange animal, is universal. It has been disco- vered to exist in every nation and to be associated with their most ancient reminiscences, without ever having ceased to be believed in. This tradition will be found clearly traced to its origin, throughout its various rami- fications, in the 4th. and 5th. volumes of the *Monde paien* which M^r d'Anselme is now publishing. We are happy to mention in this place the wonderful labor of mythological exegesis of our learned fellow-countryman.

14. — *Baus-maniero* is a rocky peak to the north of the town of Baux. This locality derives its name from the cliffs that surround it; for, in Provençal the word

baus means a cliff or precipice, and *Baus-maniero*, *Baus-besso*, *Baus-mirano*, *Baus-couslèmple*, are names still used to designate certain quarters of Baux territory.

15. — *The goat with the golden hair.* The French adjective *roux*, corresponding to the Provençal *rous*, indicates a reddish yellow, the color of French gold. Accordingly the phrases, *de couleur d'or et de couleur rousse*, convey precisely the same meaning. This is instanced by the author's describing the animal in the 2d. line of this stanza as *la cabro d'or*, and in the 7th. line as *la cabro dóu réu rous.* In the 1st. stanza of the next canto, the phrase, *l'oli rous*, occurs, which cannot be rendered otherwise than *the golden oil. — T.*

16. — *I saw a fig-tree once.* The same may still be seen vegetating over the fountain of Vaucluse. — **T.**

MIRÈIO

CANTO III

THE COCOONING [1]

When crops are fair, and when the olive-yards
Their barrelsful of golden oil pour
Into the earthen jars;
When the unwieldy waggon,
Towering with sheaves, pursues
Its jolting groaning way along
The lanes and through the fields;

When naked stalwart as a wrestler,
Bacchus comes, the *farandoulo* [2] leading
For the treaders at the vintages of Crau;
And when the blessed beverage
From the brimful press,
Between the juice-stained ankles,
Flows into the foaming vat;

And when transparent
On the Spanish broom
The thoroughly artistic silkworms climb,
Rejoicing their golden cells to weave;
So delicate they seem as with a sunbeam spun;
And when therein by myriads
They rapidly ensconce themselves;

'Tis then that in the land of Provence
More than ordinary jubilation reigns:
The *Ferigoulet* [3] and the good *Muscat* of Baume
Are then with pleasure quaffed;
'Tis then they sing and treat each-other;
Then that lads and lasses
Foot it nimbly to the tambourin.

I clearly am by fortune favored:
In my trellised arbour
Finer bunches of cocoons, a silkier bower,
Or a richer harvest,
Neighbours, at the farm I'd never seen
Since I was little, since the year of God
That we were married in.

Thus while cocoons were being picked,
And while her female neighbours
Gossiping and gathering
Were round her in the silkworm room,
Jano Mario spoke,
The honored spouse of Master Ramoun
And the fond proud mother of Mirèio.

They were cocooning. To the women
Ever and anon Mirèio tendered
Sprigs of oak and sprays of rosemary,
Within which, by the mountain odor led,
So many noble worms had nestled
With their skeins, that sprigs and sprays
Resembled golden palms.

On *Bono Maire's* altar[5],
Jano Mario again said,
Yesterday, my women, I deposited
The finest of my sprays by way of tithe.
I annually do so; for you know
'Tis she who bountifully orders
When she lists the silkworms to climb up.

For my part, Zèu, of the *Mas de l'Oste* said;
I have great fears.
The day the east-wind blew so hard,
(You'll mind the ugly day!) I'd left
My chamber-window open carelessly;
And lo, just now I counted twenty
Whitening[6] on the floor!

Taven too to help
Had come from Baux.
To Zèu Taven said: Aye better
Than the old young people think they know.
But age must torture us,
And we must groan and weep;
Then only, but too late, we see and know.

Ye giddy women,
Should the hatching promise fine,
Quick, quick, about the streets you chattering run.
My silkworms! 'tis incredible
How fine they are! Come see them!
Envy does not lag behind,
But follows grumbling to your room.

They do one's heart good, neighbour, says she;
Clear it is you've still your caul on [7]!
But no sooner have you turned your head round
Than the envious she upon them casts
A look of venom that straight burns
And knots them up. You'll *say* then
'Twas the wind that plastered them!

I don't say that has nought to do with it,
Zèu replied; at all events I might as well
That day have closed my window.
Do you doubt still, went on Taven,
Of the evil that the eye projects
When in the head it glistens?
And she looks suspicious cast at Zèu.

Fools, that with a scalpel
Scraping on the dead, the virtue
Of the bee, the honey-making secret,
Think to find! You know not
But a glaring look
May twist the unborn babe,
Or dry the milch-cow's udder up.

Young birds are fascinated
By the staring of an owl;
A serpent's gaze will geese bring down from any height
And under the fixed staring of the human eye
You'll have a worm not sleep!
Moreover from the eye of youth,
When by the tender passion fired,

Where's the virgin wise enough
To screen herself?
Here four their cocoons dropped!
In June as in October
Ever must your tongue be stinging,
Aged viper! Eh! the lads?
But bid them come, we'll see!

No! the others of the merry set exclaimed;
We want them not; do we, Mirèio?
No: cocooning isn't every day, she said;
I'll go and fetch a bottle from the cellar,
You'll delicious find it.
Saying which she hurriedly retired
To the house to hide her blushes.

Now, good friends, began the haughty Lauro;
I am very poor, and yet
My mind's made up to smile on no-one.
Should a king, Pamparigousto's[8] even,
Offer me his hand, my pleasure
And delight would be to see him
Sighing at my footstool seven years.

Not I ! Clemenço said ;
For if a monarch
Fell in love with me,
It might be that without too much ado,
Especially if he were young and brilliant
And the handsomest in all his realm,
I'd let him lead me to his palace-home.

But once I were enthoned
As sovereign and empress, in a splendid
Gold-brocaded cloak arrayed,
And he'd my burning head encircled
With a dazzling crown of pearls
And emeralds, I would to Baux return,
My own poor country, I the Queen !

Of Baux I'd make my capital.
Upon the rock on which it now reclines,
Our ancient castle I would re-erect,
And build a tower on it
Whose white top should reach the stars.
And then when I
A little solace needed,

To my tower's turret with my prince
I'd love to mount,
Relieved of crown and mantle,
And with him alone
Delightful it would be
To peer into the distance,
Leaning side by side upon the parapet,

And take a full view
Of my merry kingdom of Provence
Before me opening like an orange-grove,
And scan its blue sea stretching languidly
Beyond its hills and plains,
And watch its noble ships tricked out with flags
In full sail shaving Chateau d'If.

Ventour[9] we'd turn to, lightning-scathed Ventour!
That venerably lifts
Above the mountains cowering under him
His white head to the heavens;
Like a tall old shepherd-chief
Among the beeches and wild pines
His flock o'erlooking, leaning on his staff.

The Rhône we'd turn to next,
Along whose banks come laughing, singing,
Cities in a file, to dip their lips and drink.
The Rhône, so stiff and haughty in his passage!
Even he will condescend to bend,
As soon as Avignon appears,
Respectfully to Notre-Dame-des-Doms [10].

Then we'd the Durance contemplate:
The Durance who, now fierce and ravenous as a goat
Devours banks and bridges in her course;
And now mock-modest as a maid
With pitcher coming from the well,
Her scanty water spills while dallying
With the lads she encounters on her way.

Clemenço ceased to speak,
The pretty Provence Queen,
And from her chair arose with apron full
And went and emptied it.
Nióulano, and Azalaïs ¹¹ the dark maid,
Her twin sister, (their old parents
Kept the castle of Estoublon,)

Often to the Falabrego came.
The little imp ycleped Love,
Who is only happy when with tender
Generous hearts he's playing tricks,
Had both enamoured of the same young man.
Azalaïs the dark maid raised her head
And spoke as follows.

Lasses, for the nonce suppose me Queen!
Marseilles and all her ships,
Beaucaire, her meadows,
La Ciotat that smiles with her,
And Salon with her almonds, all were mine!
I'd say, Come damsels, country-maids,
From Arles, from Baux, from Barbentano,

To my palace fly like birds!
And then the seven fairest I would choose,
To weigh in scales
The love deceptive and the love that's true.
Come, I would to the seven say,
And merry counsel hold.
Is't not provoking.

When a couple's, well assorted
Half the time they can't be married?
But once I, Azalaïs am Queen,
I do affirm that in my realm,
If ever loving pair contraried be
By any unjust odious cause,
At this tribunal of the seven maidens,

They shall find a law of clemency.
Whoever shall make traffic, or for gold
Or jewel, of her robe of honor;
Whoso shall betray insult, his lover;
At this same tribunal
Of the seven fair shall find
A law of terror for offended love.

And when two lovers
To one maid aspire,
Or when two maids are smitten by the same youth,
I will have the council to determine,
Which loves better, which the better sues,
And which more worthy is of being loved.
To keep the damsels company,

Seven poets I will have,
And they shall write the laws of love
In rhyme on bits of bark,
Or else on wild vine-leaves;
Then sing them in the noble choir.
And just as from the honey-comb the sweetest
Honey flows, so will their couplets flow.

In such sort, under cover
Of the pines, of old
Faneto de Gantèume [12] must have spoken,
When her starry brow illumed the hill-crests
Of the Alpines and the Roumanin.
In such sort must have spoken too the Countess
Die [13] when she held her courts of love.

Mirèio now had to the room returned,
And with a flagon in her hand,
And beautiful as Easter-day,
She said, We'll now, good women, take a drop
To cheer us up a bit;
We'll work the better for it.
Hold your goblets out.

And from the wicker-covered flask
In turn the generous liquor flowed
Into the goblets like a string of gold.
I this elixir made myself,
Mirèio said, and to be mellowed
By the sun it must be left
To stand upon the window forty days.

Three mountain-herbs are in it,
And the liquor they are steeped in
Keeps the odor of them perfectly.
You'll find it to the stomach quite a balm.
But here she's interrupted with, Mirèio,
Listen : several have told us what they'd do,
Should royalty or fortune favor them.

In such a case, do tell us
What, Mirèio, you would do?
What I would do? What would you have me tell you?
Happy with my parents, well contented
In our Crau *mas*, nothing else can tempt me.
Ah! indeed, another said;
What pleases you is neither gold nor silver.

On a certain forenoon, I remember though,
(Forgive my telling it, Mirèio,)
'Twas a Tuesday, I'd been gathering sticks
And nearly had to La-Crous-Blanco got
With faggots on my hip,
When I perceived you in the branches
Talking pretty fast with some one nimble.

Who was he? they cried, whence was he?
Through the trees of the plantation
'Twas not easy to discern him, Noro said;
But if th'appearance did not cheat me
I am sure I recognised
A very clever basket-weaver,
Vincen, him of Falabrego.

Oh! the cheat, the cheat!
Exclaimed the lasses laughingly;
No doubt she had a longing for a pretty basket,
And she made the ozier-lad believe
She wanted him to be her lover!
Oh! the fairest in the land has chosen
Vincen, the bare-footed, for her lover!

This was how they joked her.
Then in turn o'er every face
A look oblique was cast.
A thousand maledictions on you, jades!
Cried Taven; *la Roumèco* [14] seize you all!
Were *lou bon Dièu* himself to pass
On his elysian way, the simpletons

Would laugh at him! Is it not brave
At Vincen giddily to laugh? And know you
What is in him? poor as he may be!
Now listen to the oracle : Before
His tabernacle God performed
A miracle; I can avouch it,
For it happened in my day;

There was a shepherd once,
He in the wilderness his life had passed
His flock while tending on the Luberon [15].
At length his iron-frame
Inclining to the grave,
He to the hermit of S[t] Ouqueri
Determined to confess, as was his duty.

All alone and lost in the Vaumasco [16],
He his foot had never set
In church or chapel since his first communion;
E'en his prayers
Had from his memory slipped.
But now his hut he quitted for the hermitage,
And to the ground before the hermit bowed.

Of what sin, the confessor asked,
Dost thou accuse thyself, my brother?
I accuse myself alas! replied
The aged man, of having one day murdered
With a stone a bird that had been flying
Round about my flock,
And is the shepherd's friend, a wagtail.

If he have no ill design
The man must be an idiot!
Thought the hermit, studying his features;
So to cut the matter short and solve the problem,
Go, said he, and hang thy cloak
Upon yon beam; then come,
I'll give thee absolution.

Glancing through the chapel was a sunbeam;
This it was the priest had pointed to
To test him! Of his cloak the good old shepherd
Soon divests himself and credulously
Throws it up into the air,
When lo, suspended to the sunbeam
Hangs the cloak!

O man of God! exclaimed the hermit,
Casting himself down
Before the shepherd weeping,
Is it possible for me to thee absolve?
Ah! let the rain now falling from my eyes
Fall on thy hand, and let that hand officiate;
For thou a great Saint art, and I'm a sinner.

Taven ended her discourse.
She'd stopped the laughter of the maids.
Laureto said by way of comment,
All this shows we musn't laugh at cloaks,
And that a good beast may be hidden
Under any hide.
But, lasses, to return. As soon as

The sweet name of Vincen
Was pronounced, I noticed our young mistress
Turned as crimson as a grape.
Some mystery there must be. Tell us,
Pretty one, how long the picking lasted?
In the company of two the hour is soon forgot,
And there is always leisure with a lover.

Haven't you had jokes enough already?
Work away! Mirèio cried,
Attend to your cocooning!
You would make the Saints swear.
There now, to confound you all, I tell you,
In the flower of my age I'll go
Into a convent rather than be married!

Tan-deran-lan! *tan*-deran-lèron!
Struck up all the girls together.
Come, she's the charming Magali all over;
Magali who held love-rhapsodies
In horror such that to escape them
Went and buried herself in
St Blasi's convent there at Arles.

Now, Noro, you who sing so well
And charm the ear at pleasure,
Sing her Magali, please, Magali who love
Evaded by a thousand artifices,
Magali who to a vine-branch changed,
A flying-bird, a sunbeam;
Who however fell in love herself at last.

O Magali, ma tant amado [17],
Noro now began, and the whole room
Betook itself to work with twofold cheerfulness;
And as when one cigala shrills his summer song,
In chorus all the others join,
So now the maids in concert
All together took the chorus up.

O Magali, *ma tant amado,*
Come to the window, show yourself,
And list awhile to this *aubado* [18]
Of violin and tambourin.

The sky above is full of stars,
Softly blows the wind;
But e'en the stars will all grow pale
When you they see.

No more than for the leaves their murmur
Do I for your *aubado* care,
For I am to the blue sea going
To change into a silvery eel.

O Magali, a silvery eel
Should you e'er become,
A patient fisherman I'll be
And you I'll fish.

Know then if you become a fisher,
Sooner than you could throw your net,
I will a flying-bird change into
And fly across the wilderness.

O Magali, a flying-bird
Should you e'er become,
A cunning birdcatcher I'll prove
And you I'll catch.

For partridges, hedgesparrows either,
If springes you should mind to set,
I will a flowery herb change into
And in the prairie hide away.

O Magali, a daisy-plant
Should you e'er become,
I'll change into the limpid stream
And water you.

Should you change into limpid water
I'll change into a passing cloud,
And thus I rapidly shall wander
Away to far America.

O Magali, if to remote
India you should go,
I will become the sea-breeze that
Shall waft you o'er.

Though you the sea-breeze should change into,
I will escape another way;
I will become the scorching sunbeam
That melts the ice and burns the grass.

O Magali, a sunbeam bright
Should you e'er become,
Into a lizard green I'll change
And drink you up.

Should you a salamander change to,
And in a thicket hide yourself,
I will become the moon that lightens
The witch and sorcerer by night.

O Magali, the moon serene
Should you e'er become,
Then to a halo changing I'll
Envelop you.

E'en though you should become a halo,
Envelop me you never shall;
For I a virgin-rose shall change to,
And bloom defiant 'mid the thorns.

O Magali, a blooming rose
Should you e'er become,
Into a butterfly I'll change
And you I'll kiss.

Go on for ever, running running,
Never, oh! never me you'll catch;
For I will in the forest clothe me
With the old oak-tree's gnarlëd bark.

O Magali, a forest-tree
Should you e'er become,
The clinging ivy I will be
And you embrace.

Though you should in your arms enfold me,
An old oak only you will clasp,
For I'll become a white-veiled sister
In great St Blasi's monast'ry.

O Magali, a white veiled nun
Should you e'er become,
At the confessional as Priest
I'll you confess.

Here all the women started!
From their hands the cocoons fell.
Noro, they cried, oh! tell us, tell us, please,
What further Magali, a nun now, answered?
Magali who had, poor dear,

Already been an oak, a flower,
The moon, the sun, a cloud, a bird, a fish!

The rest I'll sing you, Noro said:
We were, I think, where she
Was entering the nunnery,
And where the eager birdcatcher replies,
He'll as confessor introduce himself
And shrive her. Now, once more
The obstacle that she opposes mark.

The sanctuary should you enter,
There in a circle you will find,
In tears, the nunnery assembled
Around me in my windingsheet.

O Magali, a lifeless corpse
Should you be at last,
Into the yawning grave I'll change
And hold you fast!

Now I indeed begin to fancy
It is not lightly that you speak.
See, here's my annulet in crystal,
Wear it for *me*, my handsome lad.

O Magali, you've done me good.
But behold the stars!
O Magali, since they saw you
How they have paled!

Noro is silent, not a word is said.
She sang so well that sympathetically
All joined in, their heads bent low;
E'en as the drooping withies,
Flexible and docile,
By the flowing eddies of a stream
Are turned and swayed.

Her song concluded, Noro said,
How fine the weather is!
The mowers at the vivary are washing off
The grime upon their scythes.
Mirèio, pick us, please, a few S*t* John's-day apples,
And we'll go with some fresh cheese and lunch
Under the *falabrego*-trees.

NOTES

TO THE THIRD CANTO

———

1. — *The cocooning*, or gathering of the cocoons, described in the seventh stanza of this canto. — T.

2. — *The farandoulo*, a Provençal dance. — T.

3. — *The Ferigoulet*, an excellent wine, grown on one of the hill-sides of Graveson (B⁸ du Rhône). *Ferigoulo* means thyme, and the wine agreeably recalls the perfume of that plant.

4. — *The good Muscat of Baume.* Baume is a village in the department of Vaucluse. The environs produce a Muscat that is much esteemed.

5. — *Bono Maire's altar*, that of *the good mother*, or the holy Virgin's.

6. — *Whitening, canela;* this word is used to describe the silkworms suffering from the terrible disease called the *muscardine*, due to the development of a sort of mouldiness, and which gives them a plastery appearance.

7. — *You've still your caul on (as la crespino). Crespino* a cap, or the membrane some children have on their heads at their birth, and which is in the popular mind a certain sign of good luck.

8. — *Pamparigousto,* an imaginary country, such as *Cocagne.*

9. — *Ventour,* a high mountain forty eight kilometres to the N. E. of Avignon, abruptly rising, 1,911 metres above the level of the sea, isolated, steep, visible forty leagues off, and for six months of the year capped with snow.

Geographers are wrong in writing it *Ventoux* instead of *Ventour.* All the surrounding populations pronounce it *Ventour.* The name of one of its appendages is *Ventouret,* and a certain north-wind is called *la Ventou-reso* because it blows from that quarter.

10. — *N.-D.-des-Doms,* the cathedral church at Avignon in which the popes formerly officiated. — T.

11. — *Azalaïs,* the Provençal form of the name Adelaide.

12. — *Faneto de Ganteume.* Janette, abridged from Estéfanette, of the noble family of Gantelme, presided about the year 1340 over the Court of love of Romanin. Courts of love are known to have been poetical assizes at which the noblest, most beautiful, and most learned ladies in *Gay-saber,* decided on questions of gallantry and love, and awarded prizes for Provençal poetry. The celebrated and lovely Laura was niece to Fanette de Gantelme and a member of her graceful areopagus.

The ruins of the castle of Romanin may still be seen not far from St Remy, at the foot of the northern slope of the Lower Alps.

13. — *The Countess Die*, a celebrated poetess of the middle of the twelfth century. Such of her poems as have come down to us contain some strains more impassioned and occasionally more voluptuous than those of Sappho.

14. — *The Rouinèco*, a sort of vampire of the South. The Marquis Lafare Alais has given the following description of it in his *Castagnados*:

> Sus vint arpo d'aragno
> S'escasso soun cors brun ;
> Soun ventre, que regagno,
> Di fèbre e de magagno
> Suso l'orre frescun.

(That is : — On twenty spider-legs its brown body, as on stilts, is mounted ; its belly swelled with fever and rottenness, the horrid odor thereof exudes. — T.)

15. — *The Luberon*, a mountain-chain in the department of Vaucluse.

16. — *The Vaumasco* (from *Vau masco*, valley of sorcerers', a valley of the Luberon, formerly inhabited by the Vaudois.

17. — *Ma tant amado*, my so much loved. For this phrase it is hard to find a proper equivalent, and, owing to the incomparable energy of the monosyllabic *tant*, quite impossible to render it literally. — T.

18. — An *aubado* (from *l'aubo* the dawn), is music performed in the morning early, under a window, just as a serenade is in the evening. — T.

MIRÈIO

CANTO IV

THE SUITORS

In the cool meadows,
When the violets in bunches blow,
There are not lacking couples
In the shade
To go and cull them.
When the sea calms down her angry bosom,
And her billows gently heave,

There are not lacking boats and smacks
That from Martegue [1] go in fleets,
Go on their wings of oars
Over the tranquil sea and there disperse,
And with their nets inclose the fish.
And when among the women comes the swarm
Of maidens in their bloom,

When country-lasses and countesses win renown
For beauty, in the cottages of Crau
And in the farmsteads suitors are not lacking;
To the Falabrego-Mas alone
There came a trio; one kept horses,
One a herdsman was, and one a shepherd.
All three fine lads.

Alari the shepherd was the first to come.
They say he had a thousand sheep that grazed
The rich salt-pastures all the winter through
On lake Entressen's banks [2]. They say that at
Wheat-bolling, when the warmth of May is felt,
To the cool regions of the Upper Alps
Himself was wont to lead them.

They moreover say, and I believe it,
That about St Mark's day nine sheep-shearers,
Famous all, sheared for him;
Not to mention him engaged to bear away
The heavy fleeces, or the sheep-boy who
Unceasingly the quickly emptied can
Replenished for the shearers.

When the heat began to moderate,
And snow was falling thick
Upon the mountain-tops in Gavot land,
You should have seen descend,
From the upper valleys of Dauphiny
To the immense Crauenco plain,
This splendid flock to graze the winter-grass.

You should have seen this multitude
Defile into the stony road;
The early lambkins heading the whole band
Came capering on in merry groups,
The lambherd guiding them. Then came
The bell-decked asses, he and she, their foals beside
Or in disorder trotting after them.

A drover has the charge of these :
Astride upon his mule,
'Tis he who in the wattled panniers
Keeps the clothing,
Drink and eatables,
The hides still bleeding of the slaughtered cattle,
And the weary lamb.

As captains of the host,
With horns curved backward,
Jingling their bells, come on abreast
Five lordly bucks with threatening heads
And looks askant;
Behind them come the mothers
With their little madcap kids.

This greedy vagabond troop
The goatherd tends.
Then on the road appear
The large ram-chiefs,
With muzzles lifted up;
They are distinguished by their heavy horns
Thrice curled about their ears.

They have their ribs and backs
Moreover decked with tufts of wool,
In honorable token that they are
The flock's sires. The chief shepherd
At his troop's head marches
With his cloak wrapped round his shoulders,
While the main corps of the army follows

In a cloud of dust.
And hastily preceding come the ewe-dams,
Answering by long bleatings
To the bleatings of their lambs,
The little horned ones prinked
With small red tufts about their necks.
Then come the woolly slowly-pacing sheep.

From time to time the shepherd-boys are heard
The dogs commanding. Then the countless flock
With pitch-marked sides are seen, the yearling-ewes
Biennial breeders and the two-year olders,
Those whose lambs have from them weanëd been,
And the twin-breeders that reluctantly
And wearily their heavy burdens bear along.

And lastly comes
A ragamuffin squadron;
'Tis of barren and past-breeding ewes
Composed, the toathless and the lame;
The sad remains of superannuated
Worn out rams, that horns and honor
Have together lost.

And all these asses sheep and goats,
As many as the way contains;
All, young old good bad and indifferent;
Are Aɪari's:
And when before him they descend,
Defiling off by hundreds, his eyes glisten!
For a sceptre he a maple-cudgel bears;

And when to pasture going,
Followed by his large sheep-dogs,
And in his leather-gaiters buttoned to the knees,
You'd take him, with his air serene and forehead sage
For Royal David's self,
As in his youth he went his flocks to water
At his father's wells.

Why! that must be Mirèio
Standing at the Falabrego-door!
Exclaimed the shepherd-chief. Good heavens!
They have not deceived me : nowhere whether
In the uplands or the lowlands, or in pictures
Or reality, none have I ever seen
That to her waist comes up for manners grace or beauty

Only to behold her
Alari had left his flocks and herds,
And when he was before her,
Could you, in a trembling voice, he said,
Point out to me a way to cross the hills?
If not, fair maid, I fear
I'll not be able to proceed.

Thou'st only, see, to take the straight road,
Answered the *mas* maiden ;
Then thou'lt enter Pèiromalo desert ;
Then thou'lt take the winding path,
Till to a portico [3] thou come ;
A tomb is near it on which stand .
The lofty statues of two generals [3];

We call them the antiquities.
Oh ! many thanks, returned the youth.
A thousand of the woolly tribe,
And with my mark upon them,
From La Crau tomorrow will ascend the hill.
I lead the band and settle, as we go,
The feeding grounds, the sleeping spots, and eke the roa

They're of a fine breed all the beasts.
My shepherdess, moreover, when I marry
Will the nightingale hear singing day and night.
And had I any hope, adorable Mirèio,
You'd my offering accept, I'd offer you
Not jewels, but a box-wood goblet
I have carved for you and spickspan new.

.

Then as he ceased to speak,
Enveloped like a relic, from his coat
He drew a goblet carved
Out of green box-wood. In his leisure hours
His pleasure was to sit upon a stone
And with such things amuse himself.
And too, with nothing but a knife, he wrought divine

With fantastic hand he carved him
Castanets, by means of which at night
Across the fields he led his flock ;
And on the ringing collars, and the bones
That served for bell-tongues,
He would faces cut and figures,
Flowers and birds, and all he minded.

But the goblet now produced
You would deny, I'm sure,
A shepherd's knife had fashioned it.
A poppy in full blossom
Bloomed around it,
And between its languid flowers
Two chamois grazed, the handles forming.

Just a little lower down
Were seen three maidens,
That were certainly three marvels.
Near, beneath a tree, a shepherd-lad was sleeping;
And the merry maidens were advancing
Softly on tiptoe, and laying on his mouth
A bunch of grapes, of which they had a basket full.

All smiles the youth awakes :
One of the maidens seems confused.
The goblet smelt quite new.
He hadn't yet drunk out of it.
But for the color of the wood
You'd have declared
The figures in the work were living.

Of a truth, Mirèio said inspecting it,
Shepherd, thine offering is tempting.
But, she suddenly exclaimed, my heart's lord
Hath a finer one ! it is his love,
O shepherd ! and when his impassioned eyes
Are on me, mine must close ; the bliss
I feel steal over me o'erpowers me.

Then like a sprite the maiden vanished.
Alari the shepherd folded up
His goblet carefully again
And slowly in the twilight
Left the house, disturbed to think
A maid so fair, so much in love should be
With any one but him.

To the Falabrego-Mas there came besides
A keeper of wild horses, Veran called.
This Veran came from Sambu [4]. Round
About Sambu, and in the large prairies
Where blooms the *Cabridello* [5], he a hundred
Steeds possessed, all white, that nipped the heads off
Of the lofty reeds.

A hundred steeds,
With manes like billows of the sea,
Long wavy thick and innocent of shears.
And when they start impetuous
On their headlong courses
Their dishevelled manes fly up
And like the scarfs of white-robed fairies wave.

Oh! shame upon the human race!
Camargan [6] steeds have never
To the cruel spur,
No more than to the hand that flatters them,
Been known to be submissive.
Haltered treacherously, some I've known
To have been from their salt-plains torn;

But one day with a vicious sudden start,
Their riders thowing off,
They've at a heat scoured twenty leagues of country,
Snuffing up the wind,
And to their native Vacarés [7] returned
To breathe their salt-sea-air again, and roam
In freedom after ten years' slavery!

For these white horses' element's the sea!
Foam-colored they are still!
They doubtless from the car
Of Neptune broke away!
For when the sea is heard to moan and seen to scowl,
When ships their cables part,
The stallions of Camargue rejoicing neigh

And smack like whipcord
Their long-hanging tails,
Or paw the ground
As though they felt
The pricking trident of the angry god,
Who stirs the tempest into deluge
And the sea's depths to their very bottom.

These same Veran pastured.
To La Crau one day his business taking him,
'Tis said towards Mirèio's *mas*
He bent his steps. For in Camargue
And even at the wide mouths yonder
Where the Rhône debouches
'Twas reported she was fair, and long it will be.

Proudly he advanced,
With paletot after the Arlesian fashion
Long and light, thrown over both his shoulders
Like a cloak; a girdle round his loins
Checkered like a lizard's back,
And on his head an oil-skin hat
Off which the sunbeams glanced.

And when in presence of the Master,
He, Good morrow to thee, said, and eke prosperity!
Upon the banks of the Camargan Rhône
I dwell. I'm Keeper Peire's grandson.
Nay, but thou must know it, seeing that
For twenty years at least my grandsire
Keeper Peire's horses trod thy treading-floor.

Thou must remember too
My venerable grandsire owned three dozen [8].
But, O Master Ramoun! if thou couldst but see
Th'astounding increase of this little leaven!
Now the sickles may be harder plied than ever,
For we've seven dozen and as many couple [9].
Long, the old man answered, Long, my son,

May you both lead them out to pasture
And behold them multiply!
Your grandsire well I knew, and certes
Our friendship is of ancient standing.
But the frost of age has come,
And by the light of our own lamp [10] we needs
Must quietly remain and friendly visits cease.

But that's not all, pursued the youth,
And what I want of thee thou know'st not yet.
At Sambu, when the Crau folks come
In quest of waggon-loads of litter,
And, while we are helping them
To cord them down, it happens
They will sometimes of the Crau maids talk,

And thy Mirèio they've depicted
So much to my taste, that if to thine too
Veranet [11] thou find, thy son-in-law he'll be.
How, Veranet! may I but see it!
Ramoun cried; for of your grandsire,
Keeper Peire, of my friend,
The blooming scion can but do me honor.

Then, up to the heavens like a saint
Returning thanks, he raised his hands and said,
Provided you be to the child agreeable,
For as she is the only one she is the darling.
Meanwhile, and as earnest of her dower,
May the blessing of the saints
And their eternity be yours!

His daughter straightway then he called
And soon had told her.
Pale at once, afraid and trembling with emotion,
Thus she spoke, Why, father mine,
Thy saintly understanding what's it thinking of,
That young, so young as I am,
Thou shouldst wish me married?

It is slow work, hast thou often told me,
Taking to each-other. One must know
One's folk, one must be known; and when
One knows and is known, is that all?
The dark cloud here upon her face was suddenly
Illumined as by some bright thought.
E'en as the drowning flowers

After morning-rain may through the water
That encumbers them be seen to smile.
Mirèio's mother countenanced her daughter.
Then the keeper blandly,
Master Ramoun, said he, I withdraw:
For I can tell thee, a Camargan keeper
Knows the sting of a mosquito well!

There came besides to sue the maiden,
In the course of the same summer,
From the Sóuvage [12] pastures, Ourrias [13]
The cattle-breaker and their brander.
Black and wicked are the cattle
Of the Sóuvage. To the broiling sun
The cold fogs and the pouring rain exposed,

The whole year round
Alone he, Ourrias, had charge of them.
Among the cattle born and bred,
He had their build and cruel heart,
The same wlld eye, dark color, dogged look.
Cudgel in hand,
His coat upon the ground,

How often, savage weaner that he was,
Had he not from the udders
Wrenched the calves,
And on the angry mother
Broken cudgel after cudgel,
Until she, to flee the storm of blows,
Ran lowing to the pine-copse, gazing back.

How many oxen two-year old and heifers three,
In the *ferrado* [14] at Camargue had he not,
Seizing by the horns, laid low!
Moreover he'd between his eyes a scar,
Jagged like the forky ray of lightning on a cloud
And once the verdant plain was crimsoned
With his blood!

It happened on a grand *ferrado* day.
To help in mustering the herd,
Li Santo, Aigui-Morto, Faraman,
And Aubaroun [15], had sent into the wild
A hundred of their ablest horsemen.
Roused in their salt-wilderness,
Pursued and harassed by the trident

Of the impetuous brander
At full gallop, bulls and heifers
Like a gust of wind came headlong
Rushing, crashing salicorne and centaury [16],
And mustered at the branding-booth,
Where crowds had met,
Three hundred strong.

They stand a moment scared,
Bewildered motionless,
And then are goaded in their sides;
They start afresh and thrice are forced to make
The circuit of the amphitheatre;
Like marterns hunted by a dog, like sparrow-hawks
Chased by the eagle of the Luberoun [17].

Credit it who will? but Ourrias,
To usage counter, from his horse alights.
The cattle at the crowded circus-doors
Start suddenly, and five young bulls
With flaming eyes, and with their proud horns
Striving as it were to pierce the sky,
Rush into the arena.

Ourrias pursues them
Like the wind the clouds,
He goads them running,
Running he outstrips them,
Now he thumps them with his goad,
Before them dances now,
Now with his ponderous fist belabors them.

I! all the people clap their hands.
White with Olimpic dust, while running,
Ourrias by the horns seized one at last;
And now it's head to muzzle, strength 'gainst strength.
The monster's object is to free his cumbered horns,
In trying to do which he sprains his back,
And then with fury bellowing splutters blood and smoke.

Vain fury! useless pains!
The neatherd, after subtly doubling,
With his shoulder forces round
The beast's huge head,
Then roughly shoving it the other way
Both beast and Christian roll upon the ground
And of a heap lay like a barricade.

The tamarisks [18] are shaken
By the deafening shouts of
Brave man, Ourrias, brave man!
And five broad-shouldered youths hold down the bull.
Then to enregister his triumph,
Ourrias himself the branding-iron seized,
And with the metal red-hot brands him on the hip.

A mounted troop of Arlaise maidens now,
With agitated bosom, flushed too
With the gallop of their snow-white poneys,
Offer him an ornamented drinking horn,
Brimful of wine; then nimbly to the plain
Again repair and disappear, escorted
By a train of ardent cavaliers.

But Ourrias has seen but cattle to be branded.
Four remained.
And as the mower mowing down the hay,
The harder mows the more he sees before him,
So the more the battle raged
The more he, Ourrias, made head against it,
And the haunches branded of the four remaining.

Spotted white, with horns superb,
The last was browsing on the green.
Hold, Ourrias! enough, enough!
The neatherds cried. Dissuasion useless!
With his trident couched on hip,
With perspiration streaming, bosom bare,
The bull white-spotted he proceeds to charge.

Zan! as he hits him in full face
The trident shivers to bits! The wound
Atrocious makes a demon of the bull;
The brander seized him by the horns.
They start together, and together
They the flowers of the plain lay waste.
The mounted Arles and Aigues-Mortes herdsmen,

Leaning on their goads' long handles,
Watch the mortal fray.
For victory both furious and savage are,
The man the bellowing beast essaying to subdue,
The beast his master carrying off and licking
With his heavy frothy tongue the blood-drops
From his muzzle as he flies.

Misericòrdi! but the bull prevails!
The man like a vile rakeful, from the violence
Of the motion, falls before the brute.
Sham dead! Sham dead! Vain counsel!
From the ground the bull uplifts him
On his pointed horns, and hurls him through the air
With his ferocious head full forty-six feet back [19]!

The tamarisks are shaken
By another deafening shout,
And on his face falls Ourrias,
Who ever since has borne
The scar that so disfigures him.
Now mounted on his mare,
With goad erect, he to Mirèio comes.

The little maid was at the fountain
All alone that morning.
She'd her sleeves and petticoats tucked up,
And was her cheese-forms cleaning
With some shave-grass.
Female saints! how beautiful she was!
Her little feet in the clear water dabbling.

Ourrias began. Good morrow, damsel fair.
So thou art thy cheese-vessels [20] polishing:
If thou have no objection, at this limpid stream
I will my mare refresh.
Oh! we've no lack of water here she answered,
She may at the dam-head drink
As much as pleases thee.

Fair maid, continued the wild youth,
If ever thou as bride or pilgrim shouldst
To Sylvareal [21] venture, where the sea is heard,
Thou wilt not have such trouble as thou hast
Down here; for there the cow of the black breed
Is fierce and freely roams, is never milked,
And women have an easy life.

Young man, in cattle-land, they say,
Maids die of languor. Maiden fair,
Where two are languor cannot be.
Young man, they say that those who wander thither
Bitter water drink, and that the sun
Their faces blisters. In the pine-trees' shade,
Fair lady, thou may'st ever keep.

Young man, they say the pines infested are
With coils of virid serpents. Maiden fair,
We've herons, and besides flamingoes
Who their rosy mantles spread
And all along the Rhône pursue them.
Listen, young man, let me tell thee,
From my *falabrego*-trees thy pines

Are too remote. Pretty lady, priests
And maidens, so the proverb says, ne'er know
The land to which they may be called to go
And eat their bread in some day. Mine but let me eat
With him I love, young man, and nothing
More there'll need to wean me from my nest.
Fair maid, an it be so, give me thy love!

Young man, it shall be thine!
Mirèio said. But first these plants
Of nenuphar [22] will bear *colombin* [23] grapes,
Thy goad will flower,
These hills will melt like wax,
And all the world will go by water
To the town of Baux!

NOTES

TO THE FOURTH CANTO

---

1. — *Martegue* (Martigue). See note 17 to 1ˢᵗ Canto.
(Pronounce *Martegue* as if it were an Italian word,
with the tonic accent on the penultimate. — T.*)*

2. — *Lake Entressen* (clar d'Entressen) in La Crau.

3. — *A portico*, etc. Within half an hour's walk of
Sᵗ Remy, at the foot of the Alpines, arise side by side
two fine Roman monuments. One is a triumphal arch,
the other a magnificent mausoleum of three stories, adorn-
ed with rich bass-reliefs and surmounted by a graceful
cupola, supported by ten Corinthian pillars through which
are discerned two statues in a standing attitude. They
are the last vestiges of Glanum, a Marseilles colony,
destroyed by the Barbarians.

4. — *Sambu*, a hamlet in the territory of Arles, in the
isle of Camargue.

5. — *Cabridello*, see note 19 to 1ˢᵗ Canto.

6. — *Camargue* is a vast delta formed by the bifurcation of the Rhône. The island extends from Arles to the sea, and comprises 74,727 hectares. The immensity of its horizon, the awful silence of its level plain, its strange vegetation, meres, swarms of mosquitoes, large herds of oxen and wild horses, amaze the traveller and remind him of the *pampas* of South America. (See Canto X.)

7. — *Vacarés*, a large assemblage of salt-ponds, lagunes and moors, in the isle of Camargue. *Vacarés* is formed of the word *vaco* and of the Provençal desinence *arés* or *eirés*, indicating union, generality. It means a place where cows abound. It is thus that from *vigno* a vine, from *barco* a bark, from *ribo* a bank, the words *vignarés* a vineyard, *barcarés* a fleet, *ribeirés* a shore, have been formed.

8. — *Dozen* (rodo). The wild horses of Camargue are used to tread out the corn. They are counted by *rodo*, a wheel or circle. The *rodo* is composed of six *liame*, and each *liame* (lien) holds a couple; the *rodo* therefore is equal to a dozen.

9. — *Couple* (liame). See preceding note.

10. — *Lamp* (moco). The *moco* is a bit of reed attached to the wainscot in the dining rooms of homesteads, serving to hold a Roman lamp called a *calèu*.

11. — *Veranet*, the diminutive of Veran. — T.

12. — *Sóuvage* is a vast desert, also called *Petite-Camargue*, bounded on the E. by the Petit-Rhône, which separates it from the *Grande-Camargue*; on the S. by the Mediterranean, and on the W. and N. by the Rhône-

Mort, and the Aigues-Mortes canal. It is the principal resort of the wild black oxen. — (Pronounce *Sóuvage* as if it were an Italian word, with the tonic accents on the first and the penultimate. — T.)

13. — Ourrias is the Provençal form of the proper name Elzéar.

14. — *Ferrado*, a pastoral operation celebrated at Arles with much ceremony ; and which consists in collecting all the young horned cattle within a certain area, and branding them with the mark of their owner.

15. — *Li Santo* (see note 21 to 1ˢᵗ Canto.) *Faraman* and *Aubaroun* are hamlets in Camargue. *Aigui-Morto* (Aigues-Mortes) is in the department of the Gard. It was at the port of this town that Sᵗ Louis twice embarked for the Holy Land. Here also Francis I and Charles V had an interview in 1579.

16. — *Salicorne and centaury*. See note 5. to 10th Canto. — T.

17. — *Luberoun*. See note 15 to 3rd Canto.

18. — *Tamarisks*. See note 5 to 10th Canto.

19. — *Forty-six feet* (set cano), seven *cannes*. The *canne* is equal to six feet seven inches English, consequently the seven are equal to 46 ft 1 in. — T.

20. — *Cheese-vessels (fiscello)*, from the Latin *fiscella*, same meaning. These are earthen vessels for making cheeses in. The bottoms are pierced with small holes through which the whey runs when the cheeses are pressed.

21. — *Sylvaréal*, a forest of parasol-pines, situate in Petite-Camargue (see preceding note 12). A small fort, built to protect the shipping of the neighbourhood, commands this island and bears the name of *Fort de Sylvaréal*.

22. — *Nenuphar*, a beautiful aquatic plant, the water-lily or rose ; *nymphœa heraclia*, Plin. — T.

23. — *Colombin*, the name of a large and superior sort of grape. — T.

MIRÈIO

CANTO V

THE BATTLE

The *Ventoureso*[1] breeze was freshening,
The shadow of the poplars lengthening,
Still the sun had two good hours to run ;
Nevertheless to him the toiling ploughmen
Ever and anon would turn their eyes,
Longing for dewy eve to greet
Their wives upon the door-step.

Ourrias, the brander, left the spring
Revolving in his mind the insult
He had just received. Shame made him furious,
So furious the blood would rush up
To his forehead. Spite inveterate
His bosom filled. Across the fields he galloped
Muttering his wrath.

As damsons in a bush the stones in Crau
Are plentiful: with these he would have picked
A quarrel and have fought; he would have
Pierced the sun through with his lance.
A wild boar startled
From his lair, and running o'er
The desert slopes of black Oulimpe [2],

Ere he turns upon the dogs pursuing him
Erects the rugged bristles of his back,
And sharps his tusks against the oaks.
Well favored Vincenet [3]
Along the same path coming
Meets the herdsman, chafed and tortured
With resentment;

Whereas he is all smiles,
Musing o'er the sweet words
That the loving maid had said to him
One morning 'neath the mulberry-tree.
Straight as a Durance cane he walks,
While happiness peace love
Beam from his countenance.

His loose unbuttoned shirt
The soft breeze swells;
Over the stones he steps, barefooted,
Light and merry as a lizard.
Many a time in the cool evening
When the earth was wrapped in shadow;
When the clover in the fields,

Its leaves, so sensitive to cold, had closed ;
He'd come and flutter like a butterfly
About the homestead where the maiden dwelt.
Or cleverly concealed,
The little chirrup of the golden-crested
Or the ivy-wren would imitate.
The loving maiden too would understand

Who called her, and would quickly
To the hawthorn-bush repair, but cautiously
And with her heart a little beating.
Charming is the moonlight
Shining on narcissus-buds ; yea,
Charming are the summer-evening zephyrs
Rustling through the ears of corn, and causing

Undulations, thousands upon thousands,
So that like a heaving bosom
They with love seem palpitating.
Joy ineffable the chamois feels
When after being chased the whole day long
By huntsmen, o'er the rocks of Queiras [4],
He stands at length upon a peak alone,

Amid the larches and surrounding glaciers.
Faint however are like joys and charms
Compared to the brief moments of felicity
Together Vincen and Mirèio passed.
But, O my lips, speak low,
For bushes have their ears !
As favored by the friendly shade

Their hands would come together.
There were intervals of silence
During which their feet with pebbles played,
And then, not knowing better what to say,
The tyro-lover would
The common misadventures
That befell him laughing tell;

Such as, the nights he passed out in the open air,
The *mas*-dogs' bites, with which his legs
Were scarred. Or else Mirèio would
Her little occupations of the day
Or day before relate,
Or what her mother to her father said.
Or how the goat had eaten all the trellis-flowers.

Once only Vincen lost his self-command.
He, crouching like a wild cat
On the barren moor,
Came creeping to the damsel's feet.
But, O my lips speak low,
For bushes have their ears!
Let me entreat of you one kiss, Mirèio!

Mirèio, I can neither eat nor drink,
Believe me, for the love I bear you. Yea,
Your breath the wind deprives me of I would
Lay up within my blood! From early dawn
To early dawn at least, Mirèio,
Let me on your garment's border kneel
And cover it with kisses!

Vincen, that is sinful!
Then the black-caps and the *pendulines* [5]
Will go and tell the secret of our love!
Don't fear their telling it, for every penduline
And black-cap in La Crau, as far as Arles,
I will to morrow banish. Ah! I see
A perfect paradise in you, Mirèio!

Mirèio, listen. In the Rhône,
Said Master Ambroi's son,
There is a plant we call *l'erbeto di frisoun* [6];
It bears two flowers on two stems;
These stems are widely separate;
The plant grows at the bottom of the water.
When however comes the time to woo,

One of the flowers to the surface rises,
And its bud exposes to the warm sun.
Whereupon the other flower
Seeing her so fair is fired with love
And swims away amain to kiss her.
To keep clear of the impeding weeds
She finds it hard; so hard, poor dear,

Her pedicle gets broken! Now she free
At last, but dying, raises to her sister's
Her pale lips! One kiss, and then my death, Mirèio!
We are all alone! She pallid stood.
He gazed enraptured. Suddenly
He like a wild cat pounces on her. Quickly
She th' audacious arm shakes off that had her waist

Encircled. Once again he seizes her.
But, O my lips speak low!
For bushes have their ears. Give over!
Moaned she, bending now and writhing.
In a warm embrace however
He had folded her, and cheek pressed cheek.
The maiden pinched him, stooped, then slipped off laugh

And away the saucebox ran
In mock'ry singing, *Lingueto! lingueto* [7]!
Thus it was at twilight these two sowed
Their wheat, their *poulit blad de luno* [8].
They were flowery blissful moments;
Such as God to peasants as to kings
Abundantly dispenses.

One evening then,
In the vast plain of Crau,
The handsome basket-weaver
Ourrias encountered in his path.
The lightning strikes the tree
That first attracts it.
First the cattle-breaker spoke.

It's may be you, you son of a ...,
That have bewitched her, that Mirèio!
Since, O rags and tatters,
You are going thither, tell her that I care
As little for her, or her weasel-face,
As for the old clout fluttering on your shoulders.
Pretty coxcomb! tell her so much for me.

Vincen started! thunderstruck:
His heart upbounded like a rocket.
Do you want me, churl, to strangle you?
To double you in two? he said,
And with a look confronting him
As terrible as when a famished leopard
Turns her head.

His face was purple,
All his body quivered.
Better try! replied the other,
On the gravel you'll roll head first.
Why, your hands are puny, fit for nothing
But to twist a bit of ozier, or
Rob hen-roosts, lurking in the shade.

At these insulting words exasperated,
Vincen answered, yea, I do twist ozier,
And your neck I'll twist!
Flee while you can, poltroon,
My anger flee! or by St James of Galicia,
You'll ne'er see your tamarisks again;
This iron fist shall bray your bones first.

Wondering and charmed to find so soon
A man on whom to wreak his vengeance;
Wait a moment, wait young madman,
Says the herdsman; first, let's light a pipe.
Setting a blackened calumet
Between his teeth, he from his pocket draws
A buckskin-pouch,

Then scornfully resumes: While rocking you
Beneath the goose-foot [9], did your gipsey-mother
Never tell of Jan de l'Ourse [10]?
Jan de l'Ourse, two strong men in one?
Who, when his master sent him with two yoke
To plough his stubble, seized,
As shepherds seize a crook,

The plough and teams and hurled them
Over a tall poplar! And it's lucky,
Urchin, there's no poplar here.
Why, you're not fit to turn a donkey off a bank!
Here Vincen standing as a pointer to the game,
I say! he cries to split his throat,
Will you come down or must I fetch you?

Guzzling, heavy-eating, hog!
You've bragged enough upon your jade.
You flinch now we're about to test
Who sucked the better milk!
It's you, is't? beardy scoundrel!
Why, I'll tread you as a sheaf is trod!
It's you despise the virgin of the *mas*,

The flower of the land, Mirèio!
I, the basket-maker, Vincen,
I, her suitor, Vincenet,
Your calumnies shall wash out in your blood,
If you have any!
Arri, àrri! shouts the herdsman;
Gipsey-suitor to a cupboard, stay a bit;

And lights upon the ground.
Away fly coats, fall fists !
The pebbles roll.
They on each other rush like two bulls,
Two bulls that have on the rank savannah,
Where the huge sun glares,
Spied the sleek haunches of a dark young heifer

Lowing in the tall grass am'rously;
The thunder bursts within them suddenly
And both go mad and blind with love.
They paw the ground, then at each other stare.
Spring forward, charge with muzzle low,
Retire and charge again ; the air resounds
With the battering of their heads.

Horribly long the battle lasts,
For it is love intoxicates,
All powerful love that urges goads them on.
Thus these two champions fought.
Thus they upon each other fell.
The first blow Ourrias got,
And being threatened with another.

He his huge fist raises like a club
And with it prostrates Vincenet.
There, urchin, parry that ! See, man,
If I have got a scratch ! the latter cries.
The former, Count the bruises, bastard,
That my fist has made on you !
Horrible monster, count the ounces of hot blood

That from your flattened nose have spouted!
Then they grapple, bend and stretch;
To shoulder shoulder is and foot to foot;
Their arms are wreathed together like coiled serpents,
While their veins are swelled to bursting
And the muscles of their calves by tension hard.
Long, stiff and motionless they stand,

Their flanks pulsating like
The heavy flapping of a bustard's wings;
And one against the other pressing
They support each other,
Like th' abutments wide and rough
Of the huge bridge that strides the Gardoun ".
Suddenly they sunder,

And their fists are doubled,
And the pestle in the mortar brays again.
Now in the fury that possesses them
They use their teeth, their nails.
Heavens, how Vincen peppers him with blows!
Heavens, the awful hits the herdsman deals!
His club-like fists fall crushing, smashing!

But how rapidly and thick
The Valabregan's patter
Like a sudden storm of pelting hail;
While round about his foe he whizzes
Like a sling whirled round.
Now, villain, look your last! he cries;
But as he bends his back to deal his blow,

The puissant herdsman seized him by the small,
And in Provençal fashion
Tossed him o'er his shoulder
Like a shovelful of wheat
Into a field away off,
Where he fell upon his side.
Pick up, O worm! pick up the dirt

You have disturbed, and eat it if you want!
Enough discoursing, ill-broke brute!
Three rounds before it's over we must have!
Retorts the lad with bitter hate
And reddening to his hair-roots.
He, the basket-weaver, rises
Like a dragon; and, to save his honor

At the risk of perishing,
On the Camargan savage rushes
And a blow delivers him
With force quite marv'llous at his age,
A straight-out-from-the-shoulder blow
Upon the breastbone.
The Camargan staggers,

Feels for something to support him;
To his misty optics all seemed turning;
Icy-cold sweat broke out on his forehead;
Then upon the stony plain,
And with a falling tower's crash,
Great Ourrias falls!
Into deep silence all La Crau was hushed:

Its misty limits merged
In the far-distant sea, the sea's
In the blue ether. Shining water-fowl,
Swans, and flamingoes with their flame-like wings,
Came to salute
The last of the declining light
Along the meres.

The herdsman's white mare
Cropped the dwarf-oak leaves;
The loose large iron-stirrups
Jingled as they dangled at her sides.
Again budge and I squash you!
Ruffian, now you feel it's not
By feet and inches only men are measured.

In the silent wold
The conquering basket-weaver
Pressed his heel on Ourrias' prostrate breast.
The brander under the incumbent pressure ·
Struggled, and there from his mouth and nostrils
Flowed a stream of thick black blood.
He strove t'unsettle thrice

The horny-footed basket-lad,
And thrice a swinging blow
From Master Ambroi's son
Resettled him upon the gravel.
Haggard, blowing, mouth agape,
Like some sea-monster horrible the herdsman lay.
The only mould of men ˉ

Your mother wasn't, after all!
Jeered Vincen. To the bulls of Sylvareal go
And tell them my fist's weight!
Go to the bottom of Camargue
And hide your bruises, insolence,
And shame, away among your cattle!
Saying which he the ferocious beast released.

Just as the shearer in the fold
A full grown ram retains between his legs
Till fully shorn, then with a rap
Upon the crupper looses him.
With rage exploding and with dust all soiled
Released, the herdsman
Springing up departs.

But what infernal object sets him
Ferreting about the fields,
Among the dwarf-oaks and broom-bushes?
Chafing, storming, cursing all around!
What is he seeking? *I! i!* now he stoops.
I! i! i! o'er his head he brandishes
His trident savagely and rushes up

To Vincen. 'Neath the murderous lance
All unrevenged and hopeless
Vincen paled as on the day he died.
Not that he feared to die;
But by infernal cunning to be mastered,
To become a felon's prey,
Was too much for his nature.

Traitor, would you dare? he'd hardly uttered
When he resolutely as a martyr
Checked himself, for he remembered yonder,
Hidden by the trees, the *mas* of his beloved.
Tenderly he turns to it,
Mirèio, look at me! as if to say,
For you it is I am about to die!

Intent as ever upon her he loved!
O noble Vincen, noble heart!
Your prayers say! thundered Ourrias,
In a voice hoarse, pitiless;
Then pierced him with his iron!
With a heavy groan th'unhappy weaver
Fell and rolled upon the grass.

The grass is flattened, stained with blood;
Already the field-ants
Are coursing over his bare legs.
The brander gallops off, and mutters as he flies
By moonlight, scattering the flints,
To-night the Crau wolves
Over such a feast will laugh!

Into deep silence all La Crau was hushed:
Its misty limits merged
In the far distant sea, the sea's
In the blue ether. Shining water-fowl,
Swans, and flamingoes with their flame-like wings,
Came to salute the last
Of the declining light along the meres.

Away, brave herdsman, gallop, gallop!
Gallop without ceasing!
Hopo! hopo! shout green herons [13]
In his mare's ears,
Causing her to prick them
And dilate her eyes and nostrils wide.
The Rhône was sleeping on his stony bed

By moonlight: like a pilgrim of Ste Baume [14]
Who from fatigue and heat has stretched him
At the bottom of a deep ravine.
Ho, ho, ho! boat ahoy!
Ho! don't you hear? on deck or in the hold
I must be taken over with my mare!
The ruffian to three boatmen cries.

On board come quickly then, good master;
See, the night-lamp has already risen, ·
Answered cheerily a voice; the fish
Are frisking round the prow and oars;
They're lively and the hour is good:
On board at once, my master, ·
We've no time to spare.

On to the poop the villain [15] gets.
The mare swims haltered to the stern.
Large scaly fishes,
Having their deep grottoes left,
Now ruffle the smooth surface of the Rhône,
And shining play about the sides.
A care have, master pilot,

For methinks the craft is growing skittish;
Then again the speaker, foot to stretcher,
Like a withy bends the oar.
Awhile ago I noticed it: I tell thee
We've an evil freight on board,
Replied the pilot, then was silent.
Rolled and reeled the old craft

Pitched and staggered like a drunkard;
She was crazy, rotten were her timbers.
Tron de Diéu! cried the brander,
Seizing on the helm to stay himself.
The craft, due to some cause occult,
Writhed like a snake whose back
A shepherd with a stone has broken.

Why all this commotion, comrades?
Are you bent on drowning me?
Appealed the brander, pale as plaster.
I can't hold the craft,
The pilot said; she springs about
And wriggles like a carp.
Villain! you've murdered some one!

I! who told you that?
May Satan drag me to the bottom
With his pitchfork if I have!
The pilot blandly then pursued:
Ah! I am wrong; I had forgot;
St Medard's night this is, on which return
To land from th' horrible pits

The gloomy depths, all poor drowned folk,
However deep in water buried.
Lo, the long procession has already started!
There they are, poor weeping souls!
Behold them on the shingly shore!
They rise bare-foot: the turbid liquid
In large drops is falling

From their mud-soiled clothes and from their matted
As in the shade of the tall poplars
They defile with lighted tapers in their hands.
Another rises ever and anon
Rejoicing to climb the river's bank.
'Tis these who like a tempest beat and toss
The craft about in this wild manner,

Their cramped legs and arms all mottled
And their heads still covered with the weeds
Struggling to free. See how they hwatc the stars!
How they inhale the limpid air,
And thrill at sight of Crau,
And scent the harvest odors, revelling
In their liberty of motion

With the water raining from their garments.
Ever and anon another rises
From the river's bed. Here come, pursued
The master of the craft, the aged men
And women, and the young. See how they dash
The mud-clots off their clothes! You forms, gaunt toot
In what horror do they fishing hold!

Fishers who caught the lamprey and the perch,
And who have food become for perch and lampreys.
Now behold another troop defiling
All discons'late on the shingle:
They are maidens fair and loving,
Who, abandoned by their lovers,
In despair besought the Rhône

For hospitality, and in the river
Drowned their grief immense.
Ah! me, alas! poor souls, they moan
So piteously, and heave so painfully
Their weed-encumbered bosoms, that I question
Whether it be water dripping
From their veils of hair or bitter tears!

The pilot ceased.
The souls had each a light,
And followed silently the river's bank.
The flying of a moth might have been heard.
Why, master pilot,
They seem seeking something in the gloom!
Cried the Camargan all aghast.

And so they are, poor things!
See how from side to side they turn their heads.
It is the good works
And the acts of faith
They sowed on earth they're seeking.
And as sheep run to the clover,
When these spy the object of their hope

They hasten up to it, and culled,
The good work or the act of faith becomes
A flower in their hand ! and when the crop's
Enough to make a bouquet, joyously to God
They tender it, when they are by the flowers
To St Peter's gate conveyed. Thus to those
Fallen into Death's huge jaws by drowning,

God himself a respite grants in which
They may redeem themselves. But ere the day dawn
Many will return to bury them anew
Beneath the gloomy river's liquid mass ;
Devourers of the needy,
Atheists, traitors, *murderers*,
And all the rest of the worm-eaten herd.

These also seek some saving deed ;
But in the gravel of the river find
But heavy sins and crimes in shape of stones,
'Gainst which they stumble with their naked feet.
The mule when dead is further beating spared ;
But heaven's pardon these shall 'neath
The roaring wave in vain implore for ever.

Ourrias here, the pilot's shoulder clutching
Like a robber at a turning, cries,
There's water in the hold !
The bucket's there ! replies the pilot coolly.
Ourrias sets to baling out as for his life,
And he toils bravely. But on
Trincataio bridge ¹⁶, that night, the *Trèvo* ¹⁷ danced !

Bale, Ourrias, brave man, bale away!
The mare to break her halter madly striving,
What's the matter, Blanco?
Asks her master, hair on end!
Are you afraid too of the dead?
Meanwhile the surge is rising,
Rises to the gunnel, plashes over!

Captain, I can't swim!
The craft is sinking, can you save her?
No! and in the twinkle of an eye she'll sink!
But from the river's bank a cable
Will be heaved us by the dead,
The dead that so alarm you.
And the vessel foundered in the Rhône.

The pale lamps
In the murky distance,
Trembling in the hands of the poor drowned,
Now cast a ray of light as bright as lightning
Quite across the river.
Then, as you've observed a spider
In the morning spin a thread and glide along it,

So these fishers, who were *Trèvo*,
Caught the brilliant beam
And swooped along it.
From the gurgling water's midst too
Ourrias his hands extended to the cable!
But on *Trincataio* bridge that night
The *Trèvo* danced.

NOTES

TO THE FIFTH CANTO

———

1. — The *Ventoureso*, a certain N. wind. See on the subject the poet's note 9 to 3rd canto. — **T.**

2. — *Oulimpe* (Olympe), a lofty mountain on the boundary-line of the Var and Bouches du Rhône.
(Pronounce the final of *Oulimpe*. — **T.**)

3. — *Vincenet*, the diminutive of Vincen, as Veranet of Veran. See note 11 to 4th canto. — **T.**

4. — *Queiras* (Queyras), a valley of the upper Alps.
(Pronounce the *Quei* of Queiras, as the Italian word *quei*. — **T.**)

5. — *Penduline, motacilla pendulina*.

6. — *L'erbeto di frisoun* (*valisneria spiralis*, Lin.), a plant found in the Rhône and in the marshes round about Tarascon and Arles.

7. — *Linguelo*, a word untranslatable into French, repeated laughingly to another while holding something tempting out of reach.

8. — *Poulit blad de luno* (pretty moon-wheat). *Faire de blad de luno* signifies literally to rob parents of their wheat by moonlight. Figuratively it is used to mean love-making on the sly.

9. — *The goose-foot* (*l'ourse*), *chenopodium fruticosum*, Lin., a plant commonly found by the sea-shore.

10. — *Jan de l'Ourse*, a storybook-hero, a Hercules of Provence, to whom many exploits are attributed. He was son to a shepherdess and a bear, and had for comrades in his exploits two adventurers of fabulous strength. The name of one was Arrache-Montagne, and of the other Pierre-de-Moulin. Mr Hippolyte Babou has given the history of Jan de l'Ours in his Païens innocents. (Pronounce the final of *Ourse*, making of the word two syllables. — T.)

11. — *The huge bridge*, the Roman antiquity known as the Pont du Gard.

12. — *A sea-monster* or sea-devil, a hideous fish.

13. — *A green heron*, *ardea viridis*, Lin.

14. — *Sainte Baume*, a celebrated grotto in the midst of a virgin-forest near St Maximin (Var), to which St Magdalen used to repair to do penance. (See XI canto.)

15. — *The villain* (*lou fena*), in French a *mauvais sujet*, *sacripant*, *scélérat*, Horace speaking of a like

character says, *Fenum habet in cornu*. This was a proverb among the Romans, originating in the ancient custom of enveloping the horns of dangerous bulls with hay as a sign that they were to be avoided.

16. — *Trincataio*, a suburb of Arles in Camargue, and united to the town by a bridge of boats.

17. — *The Trèvo (li Trèvo)*, sprites that are said to dance on the tips of waves by the light of the sun or moon.

MIRÈIO

CANTO VI

THE WITCH

The cheery voices of the feathered choir
Await the first clear streaks of morn.
Th'enamoured earth, of freshness redolent,
Awaits the sun. E'en as the maid
Attired in her most becoming robes,
Persuaded to elope, the youth awaits
Who urged their speedy flight.

Three swineherds Crau were traversing
On their return from Saint Chamas,
Ycleped the wealthy, where the mart is held.
Their herds they had disposed of,
And their money-bags were slung
Over their shoulders covered by their cloaks.
They chatted as they walked.

When suddenly one of the three cries, Silence!
Comrades, there's a sound of moaning
In the heather. *Hòu!* quoth the others,
It's Maussano's[1] or St Martin's tolling,
Or the *tremountano*[2] wind
The branches of the dwarf-oaks swaying.
Hardly was this said when they were all

Arrested by a moan so piteous
It rived the heart. *Jeuse Maïa!*
They exclaimed, There's been foul play!
They crossed themselves, then gently bent their steps
Towards the spot from whence the sound proceeded.
What a spectacle! There Vincen lay,
His face supine upon the stony grass,

The grass all gory, the ground trampled,
Scattered o'er with willow-rods, his shirt
To ribbons torn, his bosom pierced.
Abandoned on the moor, the stars
For only company, the poor lad there
Had passed the night. The light of humid early
Morning falling on and opening his lids

Revived the life fast ebbing from his veins.
The three Samaritans their homeward way
Forsaking o'er him bend, a hammock
Of their cloaks they make for him, then bear him
Off between them in their arms
And bring him to the Falabrego-Mas,
The nearest place.

Friends of my youth, belovëd, valiant poets
Of Provence, who listen to my songs
Of other days: you Roumanille who mingle
In your harmonies the people's tears
The laugh of maidens and the flowers of spring:
And you, superb Aubanel, who the gloomy
And the bright of woods and rivers seek

To sooth your heart consumed by dreams of love:
And you, Crousillat, who confer
Upon the Touloubro³ more fame than ever
She derived from Nostre-Dame⁴ her sombre
Astrologer: and you, Matthieu Anselme,
Who contemplate so pensively beneath
The trellised bower the charming maids:

And you, dear Paul, O merry joker!
And poor peasant Tavan, who attune
Your ditty to the chirrup of the cricket
Peering at your pickaxe, wistly:
And my dear Adolphe Dumas, who when
The Durance overflows return therein
To steep your thoughts, and by our sun of Provence

Warm the *Franchiman*⁵: grown up and rushing
From her *mas*, ingenuous, amazed,
'Twas you who took Mirèio by the hand
At Paris. Finally Garcin,
O worthy son of Marshal d'Alleins!
Whose soul a fiery wind burns lashes tortures
Bears away! All of you waft me

With your holy breaths, as upward
To the fair ripe fruit I climb my way.
Good morrow, Master Ramoun, on arriving
Said the swineherds. Yonder on the moor
We found this poor young man. Look out some linen
Quickly, for an ugly hole is in his chest.
Then Vincen laid they on the table of stone.

On hearing of the catastrophe, Mirèio
From the garden with her basket full
Of vegetables on her hip arrives
Distracted. All the laborers run up.
Mirèio both her hands extends. Her basket
Falls. *Maire de Diéu!* shrieks she,
Vincen bleeding! Why, what have they done to you?

The head of her belovëd she raised, gently
Turned, and gazed in consternation mute
And long, as if with sorrow petrified.
Large drops rained down upon her bosom.
Vincen knew the hand that held him
Was the loving maiden's. In a dying
Whisper, Oh! he cried, have pity!

Lou bon Diéu's company I need.
I'm greatly to be pitied. Let them with,
Here Master Ramoun said, a drop
Of *agriotat*[6] your palate moisten.
Drink some now, it will revive you.
Quick the cup his daughter seized, and drop
By drop she made him drink, and talking to him

Eased his pain. From like misfortunes
God preserve you, Vincen said, and all your care
Repay. He wouldn't say it was for her
He'd fought and fallen. Splitting ozier on my breast
The knife was oversharp and slipping pierced it.
But he to the subject of his love
Returned as flies to honey.

The anguish on thy face depicted is,
Said he, to me more bitter than my wound.
The pretty basket we began together
Must remain unfinished. For my part,
Mirèio, I'd have liked, I know, to see it
Full of thy love! Stay and let me drink
More life's elixir from thine eyes.

Oh! if thou couldst do something
For the basket-weaver yonder,
My poor father, worn with age and labor?
In despair, Mirèio bathes his wound,
Others prepare the lint, some to the Alpine
Run for herbs medicinal.
When, To the Fairies' cavern bear him!

In the vale of hell [7]!
Jano Mario cries, More potent
Is the Witch the more the hurt
Is dangerous. Four bear him forth.
There is a spot, among the rocky ramparts
Of the hills of Baux, to which the vultures
As they sweep around it point.

It is a hole flush with the rock,
Among the tufts of rosemary concealed,
By salamanders haunted. Ever since
The tongue of holy Angelus, in honor
Of the Virgin, strikes the sounding metal
Of the basilics, the antique fairies
Have been forced to shun the splendor

Of the orb of day within its depths.
They used, these light mysterious little spirits,
In and out between the forms of matter
To meander. - Half terrestrial
Created, that the souls perceptible
Of nature they might be. Created female
That they might assuage the savagery

Of primal man. So fair however
Did the sons of men appear in fairies' eyes
That they became enamoured of them,
And the foolish ones, instead of raising
Mortals to celestial spheres, inflamed
With human passions into our obscure
Condition fell, as birds fall fascinated

From their heights.
The bearers by this time had Vincen
Gently lowered down the narrow
Rocky funnel leading to the cavern.
But no one into the dismal passage with him
Venture durst, except Mirèio, who
To God his soul commended as they went.

They reached the bottom where they found a grotto
Vast and chilly. In the centre Taven sat
With body bent, Taven the Witch,
In meditation and deep melancholy,
Holding in her hand a sprig of brome.
Poor serviceable little herb! Some people
Call you devil's wheat, she mumbled out;

Yet you are one of God's own signs.
Mirèio trembling scarcely had begun   .
To tell the object of their visit, when,
I knew it! cried the Witch, her head still bowed.
The brome again addressing she pursued,
Poor little flower of the field! the flocks
Your leaves and pedicles the whole year browse

And trample, yet the more they trample you
The more your fibres multiply and clothe
The north and south with verdure.
Taven ceased. A feeble light
Was in a snail's shell set, whose flicker
Checkered the dank wall of rock with lurid light.
Upon a forkèd perch a raven roosted

Side by side with one white hen.
A sieve hung to the wall.
Abruptly now the Witch, and as if tipsey,
Cries, and what care I whoe'er you be!
Faith with her eyes shut walks and Charity
Blindfold, and neither from her even tenor swerves.
Say, basketman of Valabrego, have you faith?

I have. Then follow in my wake!
Eagerly as a she-wolf lashing with her tail
Her flanks, the Witch into a hole descends
And disappears, preceded by the croaking
Raven and the cackling fowl. With terror
Through the fearful gloom the Valabregan
And Mirèio follow her. Nay, linger not,

She cried, the time is come to wreath our garlands
Of mandragora! Obedient to the voice
Commanding them the couple never parting
Groping stooping wend their way
Through the infernal passage leading
To a grotto larger than the former.
Lo, said Taven pointing, my lord

Nostradamus' [8] holy plant, the golden bough,
St Joseph's staff and Moses' magic rod!
She said, then reverently kneeling crowned it
With her chaplet. Rising from her knees,
'Tis time, she cried, to wreath our heads with mandrake,
Whereof, from the small plant growing
In the cleft of rock, she plucks three sprigs,

First wreaths her own head, next the young man's
And the maid's; then, Forward! crying,
Down the haunted passage hies.
A troop of shining beetles march before
To light her steps.
Turning, sententiously she says,
Young people, every road to glory has

Its purgatory bit. So courage!
We the horrors of, *I! i!*
The *Sabatori* [9] are about to traverse.
As she said this, came a rush of wind
That cut their faces and their breathing stopped.
Lie down! lie down! This is the triumph
Of the *Fouletouns* [10] *!*

The countless vagabond swarm came yelping
Whirling on, all of a sudden,
Like a white squall fraught with hail.
As it blew over the three mortals were
With perspiration drenched, and cold too
From the fanning of the icy pennons
Of the sprites. Away, or stand aside!

Taven exclaimed, ye harvest-spoiling
Unlicked whelps, ye malapert curs! To think
We must make use of such as you
To do the good we do! Yea, even as
The sage physician extracts good from evil
We must too compel, by witchcraft, evil
To engender good. For we are witches.

Nought is hidden from our vision.
Where the vulgar see a stone, a whip,
A malady, an antler, only,
We discern a force at work within
Like that beneath the scum of wine
In fermentation. Pierce the vat,
The liquor boiling will flow out.

Discover if you can the key
Of Solomon! Speak to the mountain
In its language, and at your command it shall
Into the valley roll!
Meanwhile they lower, lower still, descended.
Now a roguish little voice
Piped like a goldfinch, *Hoi! hoi!*

Gossip Taven! Aunty Jano spins,
And winds off night and day.
(She thinks she's spinning worsted,
But she's only spinning hay!)
E zòu! granny, spin away!
As with the neighing of a fresh-weaned colt
The air resounded with his laughter.

Why, what's *that* voice, asked Mirèio,
Singing laughing jeering so? *Hoi!*
Piped again the childish little treble;
Who is this so pretty? Let me lift
Your neckerchief, a little raise it only.
Are there nuts, pomegranates, under it?
I wonder! Here the poor maid would have cried out

I! but Taven interposed with, Hush!
Fear not: it is a *Glàri.* Up to any
Lark is he. His name is
Esperit Fantasti.
In his better moods he'll sweep your kitchen,
Mind your fire and turn your roast,
Triple the number of your eggs.

But only let a whim possess him
And a very trouble-the-house is he.
He'll put a peck of salt into your broth.
He'll blow your light out ere you're half in bed.
Or if to Sant-Trefume [11] vespers
You be going, he'll or hide away
Or spoil your sunday-dress.

Now hear her! hear the old hag!
Hear the shriek of the ill-greased block,
Sharply replies the imp. O withered olive,
Yea, I do o'nights the bedclothes
Of the sleeping maids twitch off.
I see them start with fear and tremble
And their bosoms heave. I see ...

And off the sprite went with his laugh.
For a brief space the witcheries were stayed
Beneath the grots, and in the gloomy silence
On the cristal ground the dripping
From the vaulted roof was heard at intervals.
Now in the semi-darkness a tall form
All white, that had been sitting on a ledge of rock,

Was seen to rise and stand up with one arm
Akimbo. As a quartz-rock motionless,
From terror, Vincen stood;
And had a precipice been possible
In such a place, Mirèio would
Have plunged into it headlong.
What now! lengthy scarecrow! Taven cried,

What mean you, say, by swaying to and fro
Your limp head like a poplar?
Then she, turning to the twain half dead
With terror, said, My dears, of course you know
The Laundress? Common people take her
When they see her perched on Mount-Ventour
To be a long white cloud. Not so the shepherds.

When they see her speedily they pen their sheep.
The Laundress of destruction well they know
About her draws the truant clouds
And beats them furiously, then wrings out
Bucketsful of rain and flame.
The neatherds also to the stable
Drive their cattle hastily.

And on the angry tossing sea
The seamen to the care of Nostro-Damo [12]
Recommend their ships.
A most discordant din her speech arrests here.
Mewling, caterwauling, latches rattling,
Whimpering, and words half uttered
That the devil only understands.

Dzin! dzin! Poun! poun!
On what fantastic caldron is that hammering?
Whence those shrieks of laughter, and those wails
As of a woman in her pangs? That yawning,
Louder howling, and the gibbering,
And those groans? Give each a hand
That I may hold you both! Take care

The magic garlands fall not from your heads.
Between their legs now rushes something
Squeaking, grunting, puffing, snorting,
Like a herd of swine.
'Neath snowy sheets when nature slumbers
On a cold bright night, the fowlers,
Torch in hand, the trees and bushes

By the riverside shake well and beat ;
When all the birds at roost awakened
From their sleep fly off in panic-fright,
And with a blast as of a smithy-bellows
Rush into the net. So drove the charmer
The foul herd away into the outer-darkness
With her sieve; with which she also

Circles traced, and divers other figures
Luminous and colored like the kermes.
I! waste-layers, locusts, *arri!*
Quit my sight or woe betide you !
Artizans of evil, in your burrows hide
Away again! For you it's much too light,
Ye bats ! well by the stinging in your flesh

Ye know the sun's still shining on the Alpine.
To the angles of the rocks return
And hang yourselves ! Away they flit on all sides,
And the noises gradually cease.
Of phantoms, Taven turning to the couple
Noticed, this is the resort so long
As on the ploughed lands and the fallows gleams

The daylight. But no sooner has this
Vanished, than the lamps self-kindle
In the empty churches triply locked.
The bells begin to peal, or toll
Prolongëd knells. The pavement flags
Start up, the dead arise and kneel,
A priest as pale as they says mass,

The gospel reads. The screech-owls know it, ask them.
Ask them, when the steeples they descend
To drink the oil from the lamps
On winter-evenings, if I lie? and if
The minister who pours the wine
Into the holy cup is not, of all
Partaking of the rite, the only one alive?

Women, be careful not on chair-backs
To repose your heads too long and fall asleep,
Especially about the time
The *Vièio* jeers. What time
The *Vièio* February jeers [13],
Your charges, shepherds, hurdle earlier
Than usual, an ye heed not to remain

Aghast and seven years spell-bound with your sheep
And stiff of limb. The Fairies' cavern looses
Too at this time all its horde, to roam
On all-fours or to fly about in Crau;
Whither repair likewise by devious ways
The wizards of Varigoulo [14]
And Fanfarigoulo [15] magicians,

Who the golden tankard quaff and dance
The *farandole*. Behold the Garrigo [16]
Are dancing it already. How they foot it!
Fretting with impatience too observe
The Garamaude [17] awaiting the Gripet [18].
Ah! heartless flirt, fie! Bite the carrion, Gripet,
Claw her bowels out! They disappear:

No, here they are again! the Chauco-Vièio
Foremost; she who down the chimney comes
At night, and stealthily upon the bosom
Gets of him or her asleep, and crouching
Presses on it with a tower's weight,
And then into the sleeper's mind instills
All sorts of horrid dreams.

She you see stealing
Through the sea-kale yonder, dodging like
A burglar as she flies, is Bambarouche
The harridan. Upon her hard bald pate
She bears off little naked crying children
Tightly griped in her fierce talons.
Hark! that clatter as of doors and windows

Being from their hinges wrenched
Is by the Escarinche [19] made in beating
All the fields of Marmau and of Barban [20]
On the moor a fog to raise. The Dra [21]
Rush up by dozens from the Cevennes with their
Salamander paunches, and in passing,
Pataflou! unroof the homesteads.

Moon, O Moon! what dire offense
Has angered you? to scowl so red on Baux!
The dog that bays beware of. He will snap you,
Foolish Moon, and bolt you like a cake!
The dog that bays the moon is Cambal's [22].
I! the holm-oaks bow their heads and bend
Their boughs like fern-leaves, and the ambient flames

Of St Elme's wild-fire [23] leap, while the mad gallop
Of the Baron Castihoun [24] makes sterile Crau
Ring with the clatter of his horse
As with a peal of bells. The Baux witch,
Hoarse and out of breath, a moment paused.
Then, Cover yourselves up! she cried,
Quick cover eyes and ears, the black lamb hails us!

What! that baaing lambkin? Vincen ventured;
But she, Shut your eyes and ears!
Woe to the stumbler here! Sambuco's [25] path
Less dangerous is than that of the black Horn.
He has, as you've just heard, a honeyed tongue,
A tender bleat, alluring to wayfarers.
Heedless Christians turning at his call

He dazzles with the sheen of Herod's court,
Of Judas' gold, and shows the place
The Saracens confined the golden goat to,.
Which till death they milk, milk
To their hearts' content. But only let them
When the rattle's in their throats
The holy sacrament demand,

And savagely the black ram butts them
In the ribs by way of answer.
Yet so rooted is the evil
Of the times, innumerable are the souls,
Greedy of gain, alas!
Who swallow down the black lamb's bait,
And incense offer to the golden goat.

The white hen crowed three shrill unearthly crows.
My children, we are come,
Resumed the beldam, to the thirteenth grotto.
They, Mirèio and the weaver, saw beneath
A huge wide chimney, warming at the hearth,
Seven black cats, all toms. Above the hearth,
And hanging to a hook they saw

An iron-caldron of vast size;
They also saw two firebrands, dragon-like,
Up to the caldron belching blue flame.
Are the logs you use to cook your boil with,
Grandmother, the same as those?
They are, my son; they're branches of the wild vine,
Better far than any logs for burning.

Vincen shrugged his shoulders. Branches!
Branches you may call them. But
This is no place for joking. Hurry on.
A large round porphyre table
In the middle of this grotto stood.
And from the grotto stretch beneath the roots
Of oaks, 'neath the foundations of the mountains,

Thousands of transparent columns,
Pendent icicles resembling,
Forming the galleries immense the fairies
Have constructed. Here are porticoes
Majestic, which a hazy sort of light
Pervades; a marvellous collection
Of fine palaces, of temples,

Peristyles and labyrinths, as never
Babylon nor Corinth equalled.
All which with a breath a fairy
Can dissolve at pleasure. Here,
Like flickering rays of light, they wander
In the shady walks of this serene
Chartreuse, their life of love pursuing

With the knights they'd formerly enchanted.
Silence! Peace be to all couples
Choosing shady walks.
The Witch now ready both arms lifts
Over her head, then lowers them to the ground.
Vincen lay speechless with his wound agape
Upon the porphyre-table; like St Laurence,

Holy martyr. Taven's spirit seemed
At work within her mightily, and grown
In stature too she seemed as upright standing
She the ladle seized and plunged it
To the bottom of the caldron
Boiling over in large bubbles, while
The cats about her formed a ring.

The venerable Witch then with her hand,
Her left, scalds Vincen's bosom with the mixture
Boiling-hot, and charms away
The cruel hurt, as gazing at him fixedly
She murmurs, Christ is born is dead is risen,
Christ shall rise again! while with her toe-nail
Thrice upon the quivering flesh she imprints

The cross' sign. Much as the forest-tigress,
Having coursed her victim down,
Unmercifully claws it.
Now her words tumultuously flow
And reach the misty portals of futurity.
Yea, he shall rise again! I see him
In the distance rising, and his forehead

Bleeding heavy drops, amid the stones
And thistles of the hill. Amid the thistles
And the stones he mounts; his cross
O'erpowers him. Where is Veronica
To wipe the drops of blood away?
The good man of Cyrene, where is he
To support him when he faints? Where are

The weeping hair-dishevelled Marys? No one!
And yet yonder rich and poor behold him
Mount, and mutter, Whither goes he
With his shouldered beam? for ever climbing
Without ceasing! Cain's descendants,
Carnal souls! with no more pity
For the bearer of the cross than for the cur

They see his master stoning wantonly.
Ah! race of Jews, that fiercely bite the hand
That feeds you, while ye lick the one that flogs you
To the marrow. Ye will have it so.
Accordingly all horrors shall assail you.
All your jewels into dust shall crumble;
What were pulse and wheat shall turn to ashes

In your mouth -and scare your hunger.
Heaps of carrion I see
The torrents foaming over!
Oh! the many swords, the many lances!
Peace be to thy waves, O stormy sea!
I! Peter's antique bark has gone to wreck
Upon the senseless rocks!

Nay, but the man-fisher has quelled
The rebel-waves, and in a fine new bark
The Rhône is entering with God's cross
Upon her poop! Rainbow divine!
O clemency immense, sublime, eternal!
Lo, another land another sun I see
Rejoicing the hearts of olive-pickers

As they dance the *farandole* around
The hanging fruit. The reapers tap the cask
Reclining on the barley-sheaves.
Revealed by signs so many God is worshiped
In his holy temple. With her finger
Here the Witch of Baux dismissed the children,
Pointing the way out. At the extremity.

Light gleamed in. Hurriedly they make for it,
And thread the passage to the Trau de Cordo [26],
Where they see the sun again. They also see
As in a dream Mount-Majour's ruins scattered
O'er the mountain. But, or ever passing out
Into the sunny air, with one consent
They turn and tenderly embrace.

NOTES

TO THE SIXTH CANTO

—

1. — *Maussano, Saint Martin*, villages in Crau.

2. — *Tremountano*, the N. E. wind. — T.

3. — *The Touloubro*, a small river that empties itself into the lake of Berre, after traversing the territory of Salon, the fatherland of the poet Crousillat.

4. — *Nostre Dame (Nostradamus)*. Michel de Nostre-dame, or Nostradamus, was born at St Remy in 1503, and died at Salon in 1565. He practised medicine very successfully under the latter Valois, applied himself to mathematics and astrology, and published in 1557, under the title of *Centuries*, the famous prophecies that have rendered his name popular. Charles IX appointed him his physician in ordinary and loaded him with honors.

5. — *Franchiman*, the term used by Provençaux to designate the French speaking part of the nation. — T.

6. — *Agriotat,* a liquor composed of brandy and sugar, with which a certain quantity of the short-stalked cherry, well bruised, is mixed.

7. — *The Fairies' cavern.* We like to quote our friend Jules Canonge because he has happily described most of the places mentioned in this poem.

« From the bottom of a gorge, aptly named *Enfer,* I descended to the Fairies' grotto. But instead of the graceful phantoms with which my imagination had peopled it, I saw nothing but low vaults under which I was forced to crawl, blocks of stone heaped up, bats and gloomy depths. I have just observed that this gorge is aptly called *Enfer.* No where else in fact have I ever seen rocks so *tormented.* They stand erect with cavities in their sides, and their gigantic entablements covered with aerial gardens, in which a dishevelled sort of vegetation obtains, defile out like the Pyrenean rock cleft by the sword of Rolland. » (*Histoire de la ville des Baux.* Avignon, Aubanel frères.)

On comparing the description of Dante's *Inferno* with this tortured Cyclopean fantastic vista, one is persuaded of one thing, that the great Florentine poet who had travelled in our parts and even sojourned at Arles, must have visited the town of Baux, sat on the escarpments of the *valoun d'Infèr,* and being struck with the grandeur of its desolation, conceived in the midst of its cataclysm of rocks the outline and sombre character of his *Inferno.* Every thing leads to the idea, even the name of the gorge itself, *Infèr,* its amphitheatrical form, the same given by Dante to Hell, and the large detached rocks forming its escarpments,

> In su l'estremità d'un' alta ripa
> Che facevan gran pietre rotte in cerchio,

And the Provençal name of these same, *baus,* italianised

by the poet into *balzo,* and given by him to the
escarpments of his own lugubrious funnel.

8. — *Nostradamus.* See note 4. — T.

9. — *Sabatori.* Besides its etymological meaning this
word is used to designate a meeting supposed to be held
by sorcerers at night to worship the devil. It is also used
in speaking of any great noise, disorderly and confusedly
made. — T.

10. — *The Fouletouns,* a sort of spirits considered
mischievous but not wicked. — T.

11. — *Sant Trefume* (St Trophimus), the cathedral at
Arles, built in the VII century by archbishop Saint
Virgile, in which Frédéric Barberousse was consecrated
emperor in 1178. (Pronounce the final of *Trefume* as it
would be in Italian. — T.

12. — *Nostro Damo,* Notre Dame de la Garde at Mar-
seilles, the patroness of mariners. — T.

13. — *The Vièio February jeers.* Peasants in the south
of France have remarked that the three last days of
February and the three first days of March are almost
always visited with a renewal of cold, and this is how
their poetic imagination accounts for the fact.
An old woman, once upon a time, was tending her
sheep. It was towards the end of February which that
year had not been severe. The old woman, believing

that she was well clear of winter, began jeering February
as follows :

Adiéu, Febrié ! Mé ta febrerado.
M'as fa ni pèu ni pelado !

(Farewell, February ! With your frost ·
Harmed me you have not and nothing cost. — T.)

The jeering of the old woman enraged February, who
went in search of March. March, do me a favor ? — Two
if you like, answered the kind neighbour. — Lend me
three days and, with the three I have left, I'll both harm
and cost her plenty.

The weather immediately after became intolerably bad,
all the sheep of the old woman were killed by the frost,
and she the peasants say, kicked against it. Ever since,
this inclement period has been known as the *Reguignado
de la Vièio*, the kicking of the old woman.

14. — *Varigoulo*, a deep cavern near Murs (Vaucluse).

15. — *Fanfarigoulo*, a valley in Crau, near Istre (B⁸ du
Rhône).

16. — *Garrigo*. See note 20 to 1ᵉ canto.

17. — *Garamaude*, the imp-flirt. — T.

18. — *Gripet*, the demon of the influenza, from *gripa*
to gripe. — T.

19. — *Escarinche*, fog-raising spirits, hollow meagre
apparitions of mere skin and bone. — T.

20. — *Marmau and Barban,* names of phantoms used to frighten little children. — T.

21. — *The Dra (li Dra),* hurricane-raisers, or spirits of the waters, especially of the Rhône, called also *Trèvo.* — T.

22. — *Cambal (Cambau),* the name of a spectre formerly supposed to issue at midnight from a sewer still existing at Avignon, called the *coundu de Cambau.* — T.

23. — *St Elme's wild-fire* or *ignis fatuus.* — T.

24. — *The Baron Castihoun,* a rattling phantom-horseman. — T.

25. — *Sambuco's path,* in the mountains of Sambuco, to the east of Aix, and much dreaded by travellers.

26. — *Trau-de-Cordo.* « To the east of Arles two hills arise which originally must have formed but one, but which now a morass separates. Upon the flat rocky summit of the lower the Celts had formerly made an excavation. It is believed the Saracens subsequently encamped upon this hill and gave it the name of Cordo (which it still preserves), in memory of Cordova. Wonderful traditions animate and poetise it (the excavation). It is the haunt of the Fairy serpent, or *Mélusine Provençale*; of the golden goat that enables people to discover hidden treasure, but who thoroughly disheartens those that do not deserve it. — The other hill, the

larger, bears the almost Roman name of Mont-Majour. •
(Jules Canonge. Illustration, 29 May, 1852).

Upon this hill are the gigantic ruins of the celebrated
abbey Mont-Majour. Both the Grotte de Corde and the
Grotte des Baux bear the name of the *Trau di Fado*,
(Fairies' cave), and the popular belief is that the two
excavations communicate.

MIRÈIO

CANTO VII

THE OLD MEN

Eyeing Master Ambroi wildly
Vincen to his father said,
(While the *Mistral* ¹, the mighty poplar-bender
Of the land, his howling added
To the young man's voice,) I've told thee, father,
O'er and o'er again that I am mad!
Dost think I'm laughing?

'Fore his Rhône mud-hut, capacious
As a nutshell, on a tree-trunk sat
The old man, ozier-withies pealing.
Sitting on the door-step was the youth,
With hand expert and vigorous, his father's
White rods bending into basket-form.
The Rhône with bosom ruffled by the wind

His billows seaward hurried like a drove
Of cows; while round about the hut a mere
Of azure water gently flowed in
From the distant waves; the willows
Offered shelter from the wind and pleasant shade;
Along the placid border of the mere
The beavers gnawed the willows' bitter bark,

While yonder, in the azure deep, brown otters
Might be seen disporting, darting
Through the limpid crystal after fish,
The silver-flashing fish.
The pendulines had hung their white nests
To the reeds and willows; tiny nests
And woven in and out with cotton

Gathered from the *aubo* [2] when in bloom.
The little warblers frisked and chirped,
And sang away the hours.
A sprightly lassie, golden-headed
As a *tourtihado* [3], was engaged
In spreading out upon a fig-tree
A large fishing-net with water dripping.

Sure the amphibious beasts and pendulines
No more afraid of her were than they feared
The reeds and willows rustling in the wind.
Poor child! her name was Vinceneto,
Master Ambroi's daughter. No one yet
Had ever bored her ears. Her eyes were blue
As damsons. Scarcely was her bosom formed.

She was indeed a caper-blossom
That the amorous Rhône rejoiced to splash.
A blockhead you must be, my son,
To speak like that. Thus with his coarse white beard
Descending to his girdle, Master Ambroi
His son answered. He retorted, For the ass
To slip his halter, sweet must be the mead.

But what's the use of words?
Thou knowest her. Her juniors one day
When she goes to Arles will hide them weeping,
For the mould of maids was broken after her.
How wilt thou answer when I tell thee she said,
You I will have! Poverty and riches,
Fool, shall answer you.

Oh! prithee, father, Valabrego leave
And promptly to the Falabrego hie
And tell them all about it. Tell them
They the virtue of a man should heed
And not what's in his pocket.
Tell them how I harrow, drive the ploughshare deep
In stony land, can prune the vines. Moreover

Tell them that their six yoke[4] with my guiding
Will plough double. Tell them I'm a man
Respectful to old people. Tell them
Should they part us, she and I will close
Our hearts for ever, her and me they'll bury.
Ah! it's easy seen that you are young,
Quoth Master Ambroi; it's *the white hen's egg*[5],

The chaffinch on the branch. You'd like to have
The pretty bird, will whistle for it,
Promise it the sugared cake, and even
To the grave will pine for it; but never
To your finger will the chaffinch come
And perch, for you are but a poor lad.
Poverty's the plague then! Vincen

Tearing out his hair exclaimed.
Why, *lou bon Diéu* who disposes so,
Who thus denies what only could to living
Reconcilé me, is he just? And wherefore
Are we poor? and why do others gather
All the best fruit of the vineyard teeming
With rich grapes, and we get but the refuse?

Master Ambroi answers with uplifted arms.
Weave on, weave on, your ozier-rods,
And tear that nonsense from your head.
The ears of corn may then rebuke the reaper,
And the worm God reprimand and say,
Peirastre [6] *!* why a star didst not thou me
Create? the ox, why not a drover me?

For he the corn consumes and I the straw.
No, no, my son; through good and evil all
Submissively must hold their way.
The hand's five fingers are of diverse lengths.
The Master chose to make you a grey lizard.
Quiet keep upon your bare wall.
Drink your sunbeam and be thankful.

But I've told thee I adore her!
More than sister, more than God!
I must possess her, father, or I die.
Then off he to the troubled river's bank
Precipitately ran.
His sister, Vinceneto, came up weeping
And addressed as follows the old weaver.

Ere my brother you dishearten
Listen to me, father. At the farm
Where I was serving was a laborer
As much in love as he. He loved
The master's daughter, Alis. Him they called
Sivèstre; and so doughty had love made him
He at labor was a wolf!

Expert at every thing, an early riser,
Quiet, economical; in peace
You may suppose the masters slept.
One morning, (see now, father, how perverse!
One morning,) master's wife o'erheard
Sivèstre talking. He his love
Was telling out to Alis.

When the men came in to dinner
And had settled round the table,
Master's eyes flashed lightning. Traitor! cried he,
Take your money, go! I've seen you.
Off the serviceable servant went.
We looked at one-another, vexed and shocked
That he should be dismissed.

For three weeks afterwards we saw him,
While we were at work,
Lurking about the homestead
With his clothes all tattered,
His face pale, dejected, haggard;
And at night we heard him as he prowled
Around the trellis calling Alis.

Sometime after an avenging fire
Bursting from the corners all at once,
Consumed the hayrick; and, O father!
From the well a drowned man was drawn up!
Here Master Ambroi grumbled out,
A little child but little trouble gives;
Grown up great trouble.

Then he goes, dons his long spatterdashes
Which himself had made in former days,
Puts on his hobnailed shoes, his large red bonnet,
And for Crau departs.
It was the season when the land
Her increase yields. It was St John's eve.
And the paths along the hedges

Crowded were with troops of jobbers
From the mountains, sunburnt, dusty,
Coming armed our fields to reap.
Their sickles, lodged in quivers made
Of fig-tree wood, were slung behind them,
By a shoulderbelt attached. By twos
And twos they came. Each couple had

A *ligarello*. Pipe and tambourin
With ribbons decked accompanied the carts,
In which reclined the weary oldsters.
O moun Diéu! what fine wheat!
What splendid tufts of ears! they all cried
As they skirted the *tousello* [7], which the wind
Was whipping into angry waves.

Won't they be pleasant reaping? How the wind
Prostrates them! But how soon they right themselves
Is all your Provence wheat as ripe as this,
Grandfather? one youth asked,
Addressing Ambroi coming up.
The red is still behind, he answered;
But and if this windy weather last

The sickles won't be equal to the work.
How the three candles shone like stars at christmas!
'Twas a blessed sign of plenty, children.
May God hear thee and bestow it
In thy granary, grandfather!
Friendly thus the woodcutter and reapers
Chatted as their way they wended

Through the willows. Now it happened
For the Falabrego-Mas the reapers
Too were bound. It happened also
Master Ramoun went out purposely
To listen what the wheat had got to say
Against the ruthless scatterer of seed,
Mistral. Accordingly he strode across

The yellow plain from north to south, and heard
The golden corn complaining, Master, see
How ill the wind is treating us! It spills
Our grain and blurs our bloom. Behold the time
Is come to put your *fingerstall of reed* [8] on.
Others urged, The ants already
At our ears are busy tearing out

The all-but-hardened wheat. Are not the sickles
Ever coming? Tow'rds the trees the master
Turned his eyes and soon perceived the reapers
In the distance. When the troop came up,
They waved their sickles flashing in the sun
Over their heads by way of compliment.
Then Ramoun shouted to the rural band

As far as he could make his voice heard,
Welcome to you all! It's *lou bon Diéu* sends you.
And of *ligarello* he had soon a bevy
Round him. Shake hands, master. Santo Crous!
What heaps of sheaves this year will strew
Your treading-floor! Appearances, good friends,
We cannot judge by altogether.

When the bushel has the treading checked,
Then only we shall know the rights.
There have been years that promised crops of twenty
Eimino per eiminado [9], and that
Only yielded three. Contented
Let us be however. Then with smiling
Visage he shook hands all round,

And friendly talked with Master Ambroi.
They were entering the path that to the homestead
Leads, when he, Mirèio! cries; Prepare
The chicory; and, *tron de goi!* draw the wine.
She soon the lunch upon the table set.
Ramoun the very first sits down at one end.
Then the others take their places.

Into bits the thickly crusted bread
Is crunched between the sturdy grinders.
Meanwhile hands in turn are dipped
Into the *barba-bou* [10].
Clean as an oak-leaf was the table.
On it in profusion set
And circulating were *cachat* [11] cheese

Truly odorous; onions, fiery garlic,
Merinjano [12] grilled, green peppers;
Stimulating dishes all.
Master at table as at labor, Ramoun
Kept the flagon by him, which he raised
From time to time with, Come, let's drink
A bumper! for the sickles keen to keep

On stony soil, must be whetted,
Often whetted. Then the men in turn
Held out their goblets. Whet the edges!
And the wine flowed from the pitcher,
Red and limpid, down the gullets
Of the reapers. Further Ramoun
To the men at table spoke as follows:

When your hunger you've appeased
And strength recruited, all of you,
According to old usage, set to cutting
From the copses branches. Bring them out
In faggots, pile them up into a heap,
And when that's done, my lads, to-night
We'll do the rest. To-night's St John's eve

And his *fête.* St John the friend of God,
St John the reaper! Thus the master
Ordered them. The noble and great art
Of managing a farm, commanding people,
And of making golden ears to spring
From under the dark sods, well drenched with sweat,
None understood so well as he.

His was a patient sober life.
In sooth long labor and the weight of years
Had bent him somewhat. But at seasons
When the treading-floors were full,
Many a time has he before the young
Farm-servants, proud and radiant, borne
Upon his horny palms two pecks [13] of wheat.

He understood the influence of the moon,
When adverse and when favorable;
When she the sap inclines to rise, when checks it.
What the weather would be when a ring
Inclosed her; when she paled to silver
Or when red became. Clear signs to him
Were mouldy bread, the little birds,

The Vaco's [14] evil days, the fogs that August ·
Vomits, parahelions, St Clara's dawn,
Wet quarantines, disastrous droughts,
Seasons of frost, and eke good-yielding years.
I've sometimes witnessed ploughing
In propitious seasons six stout handsome beasts.
It was a sight to see and truly wonderful

The soil open silently before the share
And turn its bosom over to the sun ;
And the six handsome mules ne'er from the furrow
Breaking. Toiling they seemed to understand
The wherefore and importance of their labor.
For with muzzles lowered to the ground,
And necks arched like bent bows,

They neither trotted nor too slowly walked.
Then with an eye upon the furrow
And a song upon his lips, the ploughman
Followed guiding with one handle only.
Thus went on the freehold Master Ramoun
Husbanded, and which he governed
Splendidly as any king his realm.

The chief says grace and makes the cross' sign,
And heavenward turns his eyes. The laborers
Depart the bonfire to prepare :
Some cut down branches of the sombre pines,
Others collect dry wood.
The two old men remain at table.
Master Ambroi was the first to speak.

To thee I come, O Ramoun, for advice.
I am in a predicament that only
Thou canst get me out of. How myself
I'd extricate I do not see. Thou know'st
I have a son, who till this present
Had been passing good. He'd given proof
Of it repeatedly. I should be wrong

To state the contrary. But every jewel
Has its flaw, yea even lambs
Convulsions have, and stagnant water
Is the most perfidious. Never wilt thou credit
What the crazy lad has done,
He's filled his head with thoughts of a rich
Landlord's daughter, and he *will* have her,

He says he will, the madman. His despair
And love are such he frightened me.
His folly I demonstrated. I told him
That in this world wealth increased
But poverty waxed poorer. Vainly.
Run and tell her parents I must have her,
Cost what 'twill, he answered. That the virtue

Of a man should heeded be and not
What's in his pocket. Tell them how I harrow,
Drive the ploughshare deep in stony land,
Can prune the vines. Moreover tell them
That their six yoke with my guiding
Will plough double. Tell them I'm a man
Respectful to old people. Tell them,

Should they part us, she and I will close
Our hearts for ever, her and me they'll bury.
Now, O Ramoun, that thou knowest all,
Advise me whether I should sue the parents
For the maid, or leave my son to perish?
Pòu! answered Ramoun; spread no sail
To such a breeze. Go to, not he, nor she,

Will die of it. I tell thee so much. Ambroi,
Never fear. I would not in thy place,
Good friend, distress myself so much.
I'd tell him plainly, Lad, I'd say, begin
By quieting your mind; else should you raise
The storm at last by your caprices, I'll
Indroctrinate you, *sarnipabeume!*

Soundly with a cudgel. When the jackass
Brays for extra fodder, Ambroi, never go
And throw him more, but take thy bludgeon
And belabor him. In former days
Our families were united brave and healthy,
Every storm resisting like a plane-tree branch,
Doubtless they had their quarrels. Nay we know it.

But when Christmas-eve came round,
And when his generation were assembled
Round the blessèd table which he headed,
'Neath his star-bespangled tent,
The grandsire, with his wrinkled hand
In benediction raised,
Drowned all their differences.

Moreover, Ambroi, if a father is a father
He should make himself obeyed. A flock
That takes to driving its own shepherd
Soon or late the wolf devours.
When we were young had any son
Opposed his father's will, it's more than like
His father would have killed him.

Thou wilt kill me then, my father!
Me it is that Vincen loves!
'Fore God ad 'fore our Lady
None shall have my soul but he!
Mirèio's words a death-like silence followed.
Jano Mario broke it,
Starting from her chair and crying

With clasped hands, The speech that has escaped you,
Daughter, an atrocious insult is to us.
Your love's a buckthorn that has long
Our bosom tortured. Alari the shepherd,
Owner of a thousand sheep and asses,
You refused. The Keeper, Veranet,
Whom your disdainful airs disgusted,

You refused. The rich in oxen,
Ourrias, the same you treated
For a puppy, for a scapegrace!
Go then with your ragamuffin
Through the country. Go and herd
With Roumano the fortune-teller
And Bertoun. Go with the hag and cook your pot

Under the bridge upon three stones.
For you are your own mistress, gipsey!
Master Ramoun let her say on.
But his eyeball flaming like a taper
Now flashed lightning 'neath his shaggy brow.
His anger burst all bounds and rushed
Precipitately into utterance like

A swollen mountain stream to meet the river.
Go, your mother's quite right, said he,
Take the tempest with you yonder!
Nay, but you shall not go! you shall stay,
Though I should have to shackle you
And hook you through the nostrils like a jumart
With an iron-hook! Though I should see

Your cheeks grow pale and wear away
With gloomy sickly sorrow,
Fade like snow upon the hill-sides
Under the hot sun, but you shall stay!
Mirèio, mark : as surely as that brick
Supports the ashes of the hearth;
As surely as the Rhône when surcharged

Overflows; and mark, as sure as that's a lamp;
You'll never see him more!
Then with his fist he struck the table
Such a blow as made it start.
Mirèio wept. Her tears fell thick as dew
Upon the smallage. Heavily they fell
Like o'er-ripe grapes when shaken by the wind.

And who, resumed the old man, blind with fury.
Is to certify, O Ambroi, curse it !
Is to certify that thou, thou Master Ambroi,
Hast not with thy scamp this infamous
Abduction plotted in your hut together ?
All the latter's spirit kindled. Well,
Malan de Diéu! An we are of low

Condition, let me tell thee that our hearts
Are noble ! Poverty is neither vice
Nor yet pollution that I wot of.
Forty years'good service in the navy
Tend to use one to the roar of cannon.
Scarce could I a boat-hook handle when
I Valabrego left and shipped as shipboy

In a man-of-war. I've seen the empire
Of Melinda, India haunted with Suffren,
The universe gone over as a soldier,
Done my duty in the mighty wars
Of the great warrior of southern origin,
The same who passed his red destroying hand
O'er Spain to Russia's stepps,

And at the beating of whose drums
The whole world trembled like an aspen-tree.
Apart the horrors of the boarding
And the agonies of shipwreck, I have
Traversed days more bitter than the sea.
The poor man's child who had not
In his motherland a bit of ground

To plough or dig, I for my country
Forty years of suffering endured.
We slept out in the rime
And eat the bread of dogs.
Weary of life we rushed into the slaughter
To defend the name of France.
But no one now remembers it.

On ending his remonstrance, to the ground
He cast his caddis-cloak.
Is't Sant Pieloun [15] thou'rt hunting for
On Mount-de-Vergue [16]? asked ironically
Master Ramoun. I've too heard
The thunder of the bombs
Filling the valley of the Toulon people;

Seen the bridge of Arcole stormed, the sands
Of Egypt soaked with living blood.
But from these wars returning tooth and nail
Like men, we set to laboring in a way
To dry our marrow up. The day began
Before it broke, and bending o'er the hoe
The evening moon oft caught us.

It is said the earth is generous. She is.
But like the filbert-tree she nothing gives
Unless well beaten. And if foot by foot
The clods of landed ease my labor
Has afforded me were told, the drops
Of sweat that trickled on them
From my forehead would be counted.

By St John of Apt ! must I then
Hold my peace ! or like a satyre [17]
Toil and moil in labor, eat my siftings,
That the homestead might grow rich and that
I might with honor stand before the world,
Then go and give my daughter to a tramping
Straw-loft-sleeping vagabond !

Go to the *tron de Diéune* [18] with your dog,
I keep my swan !
Such were the masters last rough words.
The other old man from the table rose,
Picked up his cloak and leaning on his staff,
But two words said : Adieu !
One day may'st thou have nothing to regret.

And may the orange-laden bark
Surrounded and directed be
By *lou grand Diéu* with his angels.
Now as he proceeded on his way
At nightfall, from the branch-heap rose,
Curled horn-shape by the wind,
A lenghty tongue of flame, round which the reapers

Merrily the *farandole* were dancing,
With their feet time keeping and their free
And haughty heads thrown back ;
The fierce flame crackling in the wind that fanned it
Lighted up their faces.
With the sound of falling wood
Into the brazier, mingled the smal music

Of the fife, but lively as the wee
Hedgesparrow's song. St John, oh ! when
Thou visitest the earth she to her centre thrills.
The bonfire crackled, sparkled, and the tabor
Hummed incessantly and gravely like
The murmur of the sea when gently breaking
On the rocks. The swarthy dancers seize

Their sickles suddenly and wave them
In the air, then thrice with mighty springs
Athwart the flames
They the *bravado* [19] do, and as they leap
They throw into the glowing embers cloves
Of garlic from a string, and with their hands
Full of St John's-wort and of holy-herb,

Which blessed become by passing through
The purifying flame, St John ! St John !
St John ! they shout. The plain and hills are lit
Alike, and sparkle as if stars were raining
In the dark. And doubtless all this incense
Wafted is by the unconscious breeze
To where the Saint in the blue ether soars.

NOTES

TO THE SEVENTH CANTO

---

1. — *The Mistral*, the N. W. wind. This wind blows down the valley of the Rhône, and occasionally with great violence. — T.

2. — *The aubo*, the white poplar, *populus alba.* — T.

3. — *Tourtihado*, a cake in the form of a crown, made of fine paste, sugar, eggs, and aniseed.

4. — *Six yoke.* « A yoke of mules outgoes a yoke of oxen, when set to work at the same time ; for mules are swifter. » *Broome.* — T.

5. — *The white hen's egg.* This is a proverbial expression for something rare precious and much held to.

Sorcerers were wont to go where several roads met and invoke the devil, with these words thrice repeated.

In virtue of my white hen !

Juvenal, speaking of a lucky man says he is *gallinæ filius albæ.*

6. — *Peirastre*, a bad father. — T.

7. — *The tousello*, a beardless wheat with a rather long stalk, the grain is large, and the bread made from it remarkably white. — T.

8. — *Finger-stall of reed.* This reapers put on their left hand fingers to protect them from being wounded by the sickle.

9. — *Eimino* a bushel. *Eiminado* is a land-measure equal to 8 ares 75, but varying according to the locality.

10. — *Barba-bou*, goatsbeard, of which a salad is made. — T.

11. — *Cachat*, a sort of cheese made by kneading, and which in fermenting acquires a sharp taste. It daily figures on the tables of farm-servants.

12. — *Merinjano*, in French *aubergines*, a vegetable much esteemed in the south; it is of a purple color and belongs to the egg-plant family. — T.

13. — *Two pecks.* The *sestié*, in French *setier*, is a measure far exceeding the *peck*, but it is also used as this word is to signify a great deal. — T.

14. — *The vaco's evil days.* These are the three last days of March and the four first of April, a period much dreaded by peasants. The *Vièio* was explained in note 13 to the VI canto. The end of the fable is as follows:
When the old woman lost her flock of sheep she

bought some cows, and having reached the end of March without damage, she said imprudently :

> En escapant de Mars e de Marsèu,
> Ai escapa mi vaco e mi vedèu.

(March escaping and March weathers
I've escaped (saved) my cows and heifers. — T.)

March in dudgeon called on April. — April, says March, lend me four days, and with the three I have remaining the old woman's cows shall not escape. April consented. A hard frost destroyed all the vegetation, and the poor old woman's kine perished.

15. — *Sant Pieloun* is the name of a rocky peak in which is the grotto to which St Magdalen used to retire.

16. — *Mount de Vergue*, a hill to the east of Avignon.

17. — *Like a satyr.* Instead of saying a man works like a negro, they say in Provence like a satyr. The ancients may have mistaken wild negroes for those divinities of the woods they called satyrs, and hence in the popular mind the two words may have become synonimous.

18. — *Tron de Diéune*, thunder of God. — T.

19. — *The bravado.* Formerly by this word were designated the volleys of musketry fired on proceeding to light the bonfire of St John. It is now applied to the preliminary ceremonies, and to the leaping over and through the flames.

MIRÈIO

CANTO VIII

LA CRAU

Who shall the mighty lioness restrain,
When on returning to her den she misses
What a Moorish huntsman at full gallop
Through the thorny brakes has borne away,
Her only whelp? Awhile she roars,
Then rushes light and lank
Over the hills of Barbary.

And who shall you restrain? O lovesick maidens!
In her sombre little bedroom
Dimly lighted by the stars, Mirèio
On her bed is lying weeping,
With her forehead in her hands. Oh! tell me,
Nostro Damo d'Amour what to do?
O cruel fate! O withering care!

O father hard, that tread me under foot!
If you could see the sad disorder
In my heart you would have pity
On your child. You used to call me *darling*.
Now you bend me to the yoke as if
I were a colt to labor to be broke.
Oh! why does not the sea o'erflow

And flood La Crau? With joy I'd see
This property engulfed and hidden
From the sun! the only cause of all
My tears. Or why was I not in some serpent's
Hole, of some poor woman born?
Then, then perhaps, if any lad had sued me,
Vincen even, sued me for my hand

They willingly had let him have it.
O my handsome Vincen!
Only if with you I might live!
I'd embrace you as the ivy does the oak.
Food to my hunger your caresses would be,
And contentedly at pools
I'd go and drink.

While thus upon her bed the lovely child
Laments, her heart consumed with love,
With fever throbbing; she goes over
In her mind the calm and happy,
Oh, so happy! spring-time of her love.
Then Vincen's counsel
Suddenly occurs to her.

,Twas you, she cried, came one day to the *mas*
And said, 'twas your own self, Should ever dog
Or lizard, wolf or snake, or any other
Prowling creeping creature, wound thee
With its fang; should e'er misfortune
Overtake thee; hie thee quickly
To the Saints [1], thou'lt surely get relief.

Misfortune now has overtaken me.
We'll go, and shall return contented.
Saying which she lightly glided off
The ltttle white cot; oped with the bright key
The wardrobe that contained her clothes [2];
An article of furniture superb,
In walnut-wood with chiseled ornaments;

Her childhood's little treasures were therein;
Her coronal put on the first time
She her *bon jour* [3] said;
A withered sprig of lavender;
A small wax-taper almost wholly burnt,
That blessed had been the thunder
In the gloomy distance to dispel.

A smart red petticoat she takes out,
She herself had quilted into squares,
A little masterpiece of needlework.
She fastens this around her waist,
And over it another handsomer
By far she slips on. Next into a black
Casaque [4] she glides, and fastens it

Beneath the bodice with a pin of gold.
Her loose hair hangs in tresses long and dark,
And covers the white shoulders like a mantle.
Now she seizes the stray coils,
And quickly rolls them up, and binds them
In a piece of fine transparent lace.
The tresses bound, she girds them gracefully

Round three times with a ribbon tinted blue;
And thus completes her fair young brow's
Arlesian diadem.
Lastly her apron she puts on
And neatly folds a muslin neckerchief
Across her bosom. *But* she had forgot,
Unfortunately in her haste, her small-crowned,

Called Provençal, hat with broad wings flapping,
To protect her from the mortal heat.
Thus dressed the ardent maid
Descends the wooden staircase
Stealthily, with shoes in hand;
Removes the heavy door-bar,
Recommends herself to the good Saints,

And in the fearful night forth rushes
Like the wind. It was the hour at which
The constellations are to seamen
Favorable. The Eagle [5] of St John
Was seen to blink as it, in one
Of the three stars in which the Evangelist
Alternately resides, alighted

At his feet. The weather was serene,
The sky with stars refulgent;
And the Chariot of Souls immense,
Its wingëd wheels precipitating,
With its blessëd load ascended
Up the shining starry vault
Towards the heavenly Paradise.

And as the flying Chariot passed
The sombre hills looked on.
Mirèio hastened; as did Magalouno [6]
Formerly; she that, so long
Disconsolate, had sought through woods
Her lover Pèire of Provence, who had been
Parted from her by the waves in fury,

And had left her lone and wretched.
At the boundary of the lea
Mirèio, in the sheepfold shepherds
Of her father sees already milking.
Some the sheep are holding quiet
By the muzzle 'gainst the pen-side,
For the tawny lambs to suck.

Meanwhile the bleating of some sheep
Was heard incessantly. Others are driving
Lambless mothers tow'rds the milker,
Silent as the night,
Astride upon a stone and squeezing
From the hard swelled teats the good warm milk.
The milk into the pail gushed,

Fast and frothy rising round the sides.
The dogs were sleeping quietly;
The fine large dogs, as lilies white,
Stretched round the enclosure, with their muzzles
Buried in the thyme.
Throughout the balmy country all
Reposed and slept. The weather was serene,

The sky with stars refulgent.
Like a lightning-flash along the hurdles
Now Mirèio passes, crying,
To the Holy Marys will no one
Among the shepherds go with me?
As when a sudden blast assails them,
Sheep and shepherds bend their heads low;

And the damsel passes like a sprite.
The *mas*-dogs knew her, but they budged not.
She is far away already,
Threads the dwarf-oaks; like a partridge flies
Over the holly and the camphyre-bushes;
Flies, her feet ne'er touching ground.
Oft on her passage, huddled in the grass

Together, sleeping at the foot
Of the small oaks, the curliens
From their rest disturbed arose in flights,
And as they flew off, *Courr'li! courr'li! courr'li!*
Cried in sombre barren Crau.
·Aurora with her dew-bespangled hair
The mountain-heights descended

To the plain and valleys. Vocal flights
Of tufted larks her progress hailed.
The summits of the Alpine cavernous [7]
Seemed moving in the sunbeams.
Then was visible La Crau,
Untilled and barren ; Crau immense and stony;
Crau antique, whose proud ancestral giants

Were destroyed by a deluge
Overwhelming, if report speak true.
They thought to overturn the Almighty
With a ladder and an effort of their shoulders.
They the crest of Santo-Vitori [8]
Had torn off with a lever and were
Piling it upon the Veutour,

As they had the huge jagged sides they'd sundered
From the Alpine. God his hand extends
And the *mistral*, the thunderbolt,
And hurricane, fly off three eagles-like
From every abyss, ravine, in Crau,
To loose the marble pile ; and rising
Like a fog opaque, Aquilo

And the thunderbolt and hurricane
Prostrate all the colossuses beneath
A vast thick covering of puddingstone.
Crau to the twelve winds open, Crau the mute,
The desolated, still preserves
Her hideous covering.
Mirèio meanwhile further speeds

From the paternal lands. The ardent sun
Makes sensible to sight the quivering air;
And baking in the grass the shrill cigalas
Madly and incessantly
Their tiny cymbals beat. Nor tree for shade
Nor beast was there.
The many flocks that in the winter nip

The short but savory grasses
Of the vast wild plain, had climbed the cool
Salubrious Alps for pastures ever green.
Still through the pouring fire of June Mirèio
Runs, runs on like lightning. And the large
Grey lizards peeping from their holes
To one-another say, Mad she must be

To scamper o'er the shingle in a sun
That dancing sets the junipers [9] on the hills
And gravel in La Crau. And in the spare shade
Of the reeds the praying-ladies [10] urge her
To return. Return, O pilgrim!
Lou bon Diéu opened hath
Springs of clear water, shade-affording trees

Created, to preserve the roses
Of your cheeks, and you your own face burn
In this fierce summer-heat.
The butterflies all vainly too
Their warning voices raised. But her
The wings of Love the wind of Faith
Bear forward on together,

As the gale the seagulls in the briny
Aigues-Mortes plains. A sheepcot
Now and then appears, profoundly sad,
Abandoned by the sheep and shepherds,
Overrun with *typha*. All alone
In the vast scorching wilderness
With neither spring nor pool

To slake her thirst, she slightly shuddered.
Great St Gent^{11}! she cried, O hermit
Of the Bausset mountain! handsome
Youthful laborer, who to thy plough
Didst harness the fierce mountain-wolf.
Divine recluse, who the hard rock didst open
For two jets, of water one and one of wine,

To flow and quench thy dying mother's thirst.
Like me thou, while they slept,
Thy family desertedst, and thy mother
Found thee all alone with God
Among the Bausset gorges. As she was
I am. So open for me, good St Gent,
A spring of limpid water, for my feet

Are blistered by the hot and stony ground
And I am dying of thirst.
In the empyrean good St Gent
Mirèio heard. Accordingly she soon
Perceived a well with a stone-cover
Shining in the distance. Like a martin
Through a shower of rain, she through

The flaming sunbeams flew to it.
It was an ancient well with ivy overgrown,
At which the flocks were watered.
By it, in the scanty shade
One of its sides afforded, sat
A little boy at play. Beside him
Was a basket full of small white snails [12].

The child was one by one withdrawing
With his little brown hand from the basket
The poor little harvest-snails and singing to them:
    Snaily, snaily, little nun,
      Quickly come out from your cell,
      Quickly show your little horns
      Or I'll break your convent-walls.

The lovely Crau maid who had dipped
Both lips and face into the bucket, looked up,
With her rosy visage flushed with running,
Now and said, Why, little one!
What are you doing here? A slight pause.
Picking snailies off the stones and grass?
Thou'st rightly guessed, the child said.

See how many I have!
I have harvest-snails, nuns, and *platello* [13].
And you eat them? I? not I!
On Fridays mother carries them to Arles
To sell, and brings us back delicious soft bread.
Hast thou ever been to Arles?
No, never. What! hast never been to Arles!

I speaking to thee have!
Ah! poor young lady! If thou knewest
What a large town Arles is.
How Arles spreads and covers
All the wide Rhône's seven months.
Arles has sea-cattle grazing on the islands
Of her lakes. Arles has sea-horses.

In one summer Arles yields corn enough
To keep her seven years. She's fishermen
Who bring her loads of fish from every sea
And river. She has mariners who go
And brave the storms of distant seas!
Thus marvellously glorying in
His sunny motherland, the pretty boy

Told of the blue sea varying rough and smooth,
Of Mount-Majour that feeds the mills
With hampersful of olives soft,
And of the bitterns booming in the marshes.
But, O charming nut-brown city,
He'd forgot to tell of your supreme
Phenomenon. The child forgot to say

Your sky, O fertile land of Arles,
Dispenses to your daughters beauty pure!
As it does wings to birds, aroma
To the hills and grapes to autumn.
Meanwhile pensive, inattentive,
Stood the country-maid. She said at last,
Bright boy, before the frog is heard to croak

Upon the willows, I must be across
The Rhône, and left there to the care of God.
Pecaire [14]! thou hast fallen on thy feet,
The little fellow answered; we are fishers,
And to-night dressed as thou art
Thou'lt sleep with us beneath the tent,
Pitched at the foot of the white poplars;

And at dawn to-morrow, father
Over in our boat will put thee. No.
I'm strong enough to wander on to-night.
Forbear! dost thou then care to see the band
Escaping plaintive from the, *I! i! i!*
Tran de la Capo? If they meet thee, down
Into the gulf they'll drag thee after them.

Trau de la Capo! what is that?
While walking o'er the stones,
Young lady, I will tell thee. He began.
There was a treading floor that groaned
Beneath its weight of sheaves. Thou'lt see
The spot to-morrow by the riverside.
For a whole month or more the piled up sheaves

A round of Camargue horses trod
Unceasingly. Not e'en a moment's rest
Had they. Their hoofs were aye at work.
And on the dusty floor were heaped
Mountains of sheaves still to be trod. They say
The sun was so intensely hot
The treading-floor glowed like a furnace.

Wooden pitchforks pitched in unremittingly
More sheaves. The beardy ears
Were shot like cross-bow arrows
At the horses' muzzles.
On St Charles' as on St Peter's day
The Arles bells rang and might ring.
Neither holiday was there nor Sunday

For the harrassed steeds. But aye
The weary tramping, aye the pricking goad,
And aye the husky shouting of the keeper
In the fiery gyrating turmoil.
Miserly as hard, the master
Of the white corn-treaders actually
Muzzled them. Our Lady's day in August came [15].

Upon the heaped up sheaves the beasts,
As usual coupled, were still treading,
Bathed in foam, their livers sticking
To their ribs, and muzzles slobbering;
When lo, a blast of cold wind blows in,
I ! a blast of the *mistral*, and sweeps
The floor ! The greedy eyes of the despisers

Of God's day into their sockets sink.
The treading floor quakes horribly and opens
Like a huge black caldron. Whirls the piled-heap
Furiously. Pitchforkers, keepers,
Keepers' aids, unable are to save it.
Owner, treading-floor and van, van-goats
And millstones, drivers, horses, all

Are in the fathomless abyss engulfed.
You make me shudder, says Mirèio.
Ah! but that's not all, and may be
For a little fool thou takest me.
But by the place thou'lt see to-morrow,
In the water playing carp and tench,
And hear marsh-blackbirds singing on the reeds.

But when our Lady's day comes,
And the fire-crowned sun to the meridian
Climbs, then lay down softly and with ear to ground
And eye upon the water thou shalt see
The gulf from limpid darken with the shadow
Of the sin; and gradually thou'lt hear
A humming sound as of a fly's wing

Rise up from the troubled deep.
Then 'twill be like the tinkle of small bells.
And then thou'lt hear among the weeds
A tumult horrible, like voices
In an amphora. 'Twill next be like
A sound of weary trotting on a hard
Dry sonorous surface; horses trotting,

Very lean, and that a swearing shouting.
Keepèr brutally insults.
But as the holy sun declines
The blasphemous sounds arising from the gulf
Grow gradually faint,
The limping studd are heard to cough,
The tinkle ceases of the little bells

Among the weeds,
And on the tops of the tall reeds
The blackbirds sing again.
Thus chatting walked the little man
Basket in hand before Mirèio.
With the sky the mountain was now blending
Its blue ramparts and its yellow crests;

And as the sun receded with his glory,
He the peace of God left to the marshes,
To the Grand Clar [16], to the olives
Of Vaulongo [17], to the Rhône extending
Away yonder, to the reapers who unbend
At length and drink the sea-breeze.
Now the little fellow cries, Young lady, ·

Look! there's our pavillion's canvas fluttering
In the wind. The poplar-tree that shelters it,
See! brother Not is climbing. He's cigalas
After, or may be he's looking out for me.
Ah! he has seen us. Sister Zeto who
Was lending him her shoulder has turned round.
Away she runs off to advise our mother

She may set the *bouiabaisso* [18] on at once.
So now there's mother stooping for the fresh fish
At the bottom of the boat. Then as the two
With equal haste were nearing the pavillion,
Cries the fisher, Wife, our Androun soon
Will be the pink of fishers, for already,
See, he's bringing us the Queen of eels!

NOTES

TO THE EIGHTH CANTO

---

1. — *The Saints*. See note 21 to the 1ˢᵗ Canto.

2. — *Her clothes (soun prouvimen)*, the provision of clothes composing in whole or part the dower of a Provençal country-girl. — T.

3. — *Her bon jour*, her salutation to the Virgin at her first communion. — T.

4. — *Casaque*, a short jacket, something like what is called a *zouave*. — T.

5. — *The Eagle*, a constellation.

6. — *Magalouno*. According to an old chivalrous romance, as popular as that of *Quatre fils Aymon*, ·Count Pierre of Provence having eloped with Magalouno, daughter to the king of Naples, fled with her across the hills and valleys. One day as Magalouno was sleeping by the seaside, a bird of prey carried off a jewel that

was glittering on the neck of the princess. Her lover followed the bird in a boat out to sea; but suddenly a storm arose, by which Pierre was driven to Egypt, where he was received and loaded with honors by the Soldan. After many romantic adventures they met again in Provence, where Magalouno, having become an abbess, had founded an hospital, around which, according to this fabulous chronicle, the town of Magalouno was afterwards built.

7. — *The Alpine cavernous*, an epithet suggested by the caverns of Baux and Cordes both being in this mountain.

8. — *Santo-Vitori*, a lofty peak to the east of Aix. It derives its name from the great victory gained by Marius over the Teutons at Pourrières in the neighbourhood.

9. — *Juniper*, the *juniperus phœnicea*. Lin.

10. — *The praying-ladies*, or *mantes (ti prego-Diéu)*. In French, *mantes religieuses*.

> « A mere professor, spite of all his cant, is
> « Not a whit better than a Mantis, —
> « An insect, of what clime I can't determine,
> « That lifts its paws most parson-like, ... »

Thomas Hood. — T.

11. — *St Gent*, a young laborer of Monteux who, at the beginning of the XI century, retired to the gorge of the Bausset, near Vaucluse, to live as a hermit. His hermitage, and the miraculous fountain that he caused to spring, tradition says, by touching the rock with his finger, are objects of many pilgrimages.

12. — *Harvest-snails*, so called because they climb up and stick to the ricks after harvest; *helix exspilum.*

13. — *Platello, helix algira.* Nuns, *helix vermiculata.*

14. — *Pecaire!* a very usual Provençal exclamation, generally equivalent to *poor thing! poor dear!* As it is here. — T.

15. — *Our Lady's day in August,* the 15 th; also the *fête* of the Emperor. — T.

16. — *Grand Clar*, a vast pond in Crau, between Baux and Arles.

17. — *Vaulongo*, a valley in the Alpines.

18. — *Bouiabaisso*, a favorite Provençal broth, made of every kind of fish, and poured boiling-hot upon slices of bread. — T.

MIRÈIO

CANTO IX

THE MUSTER

The large old *falabrego*-trees
Were sad; the bees disconsolate
Themselves shut up within their hives,
Forgetful of the heath with savory and
Milkthistle strewed; and the nymphœas
Asked the pretly kingfishers as they   .
The vivary approached, Have you Mirèio seen?

Old Ramoun and his wife at home
Together sat, their grief indulging.
Death was in their hearts.
Their eyes were swollen with weeping.
Certes, she must have frenzied been!
O giddy wretched child!
O heavy awful downfall!

What disgrace! our beautiful Mirèio
With the last of trampers to elope!
A gipsey! Who shall tell the place
The kidnapper has hid her in?
What distant cave?
O shameless daughter!
And they knit their angry brows.

Now the cupbearer, punctual as usual,
With ass and panniers came, and on the threshold
Standing said, Good morrow, master!
For the lunch [1] I come.
Go, malediction! cried the old man.
Without her I feel as though my bark
Were like the cork-tree's, stripped.

Hark ye! Return, cupbearer, whence you came,
Across the fields like lightning speed,
And bid the ploughmen and the mowers
Quit their scythes and ploughs, the reapers
Lay aside their sickles, shepherds
Leave their sheep, and hither come to me.
The faithful servant instantly departed,

Fleeter than the goats. He springs
Through the red clover-grass,
Over the stony fallow, threads
The scarlet-oaks [2], bounds o'er the skirting roads,
Already he inhales the perfume
Of the new-mown hay. He hears
The measured sweep of the long scythes

Amid the tall blue-tufted lucern,
Sees the sturdy mowers bending
To the sward; he sees the grass laid low
Before the steel, a pleasant sight;
He sees some laughing maids and children
Raking up in heaps the swath,
And they were singing, and the crickets

That before the scythes had flitted, listened.
Further, on an ash-wood cart, he sees
The mown-grass heaped up high; he sees
The skilful cartman, mounted on the waggon,
Constantly and by large armsful
Heightening the forage round his waist,
Until it covered rails and wheels and beam.

And when the waggon laboring, forward moved
At last, by two white oxen drawn,
It looked like some unwieldy sailing-craft.
The loader now stands upright, shouting
To the mowers, Cease, there's something wrong.
Behold a messenger! The waggoner's
Assistants who with pitchforks tendered him

The grass, the drops wiped from their streaming forel
And the mowers, whetting edges,
Kept their eyes fixed on the plain,
On which the sun was winging shafts.
The rustic messenger addresses them.
Attend, O men, to what the master says!
Return, cupbearer, whence you came;

Across the fields like lightning speed,
And bid the ploughmen and the mowers quit
Their scythes and ploughs, the reapers lay aside
Their sickles, shepherds leave their sheep,
And hither come to me. The faithful servant
Instantly departed, fleeter
Than the goats. He strides across the banks

Whereon the madders grow, most precious
Souvenir of Althen [3]. Every where
He sees the centaury-starred field [4]
Defloured. He sees the earth,
Roused from her sleep of winter,
Turned up in unshapely clods,
And in the furrow broad

The frisky wagtail following the plough.
Attend, O men, to what the master says!
Return cupbearer, whence you came,
Across the fields like lightning speed and bid
The ploughmen and the mowers quit
Their scythes and ploughs, the reapers lay aside
Their sickles, shepherds leave their sheep,

And hither come to me. Again the faithful
Servant instantly departed, fleeter
Than the goats. He jumps the ditches,
All with prairie-flowers bordered;
Dashes through the white-oat pieces, and is
Lost at last in the tall golden wheat.
Twice twenty reapers, like devouring flames,

Divest the land of her rich fragrant mantle,
Gain upon the field they reap like wolves,
Despoiling earth and summer
Of their golden bloom. Behind the men
The wheat falls in long files in order,
Like vine-tendrils. Ardent *ligarello*
Catch it up by handsful, under one arm stow,

And when they have enough they press it
With their knees, then tightly binding
Cast the sheaf behind them. The bright sickles
Glisten like the wings of swarming bees,
Or like the laughing ripple on the water
When the flounder frolics in the sun.
The tall sheaves mingling their rough beards

By hundreds rise in heaps pyramidal,
Giving the fields the appearance of a tented
Camp; like that of Beaucaire formerly,
When Simon and the French crusaders,
And the legate who commanded them,
Came with their horde impetuously
And laid waste Provence, slaughtering count Ramoun.

Meanwhile go about as if in play
The gleaners, gleanings in their hands; and many,
A blithersome lassie mid the Provence canes 5,
Or in the warm shade of the stacks of corn,
Is seized with languor,
After one long fascinating gaze.
Love is a reaper too!

Attend, O men, to what the master says!
The rustic herald shouts addressing them.
Return, cupbearer, whence you came,
Across the fields like lightning speed and bid
The plougmen and the mowers quit
Their scythes and ploughs, the reapers lay aside
Their sickles, shepherds leave their sheep,

And hither come to me. Again
The faithful servant instantly departed,
Fleeter than the goats. He takes
The shortest cut through the grey olive-trees,
And like a rude north-easter bends the branches
In the vine-fields. Now behold him
Where the red-legged partridges are heard,

In solitary arid Crau. Afar
Under the dwarf-oaks.he perceives the sheep
Reposing, and the shepherds with their chief
Reclining on the heather, and the wagtails
On the ruminating sheep disporting
Undisturbed. He sees a white
Light gauze-like vapor slowly

From the sky descending. Had
Some female Saint of heaven
Faint in the aerial heights,
The sun too nearly skirting,
Of her convent-veil relieved herself?
Attend, O men, to what the master says,
The rustic herald to the shepherds cries;

Return, cupbearer, whence you came,
Across the fields like lightning speed, and bid
The ploughmen and the mowers quit
Their scythes and ploughs, the reapers lay aside
Their sickles, shepherds leave their sheep,
And hither come to me. Whereon
The scythes ceased mowing, ploughs stood still,

The forly highland reapers dropped their sickles;
All came rushing like a young-winged swarm
Disturbed and lighting on a pine-tree.
Came the men of all work, waggoner
And is assistants, shepherds, gleaners,
Heapers up of sheaves, rick-builders,
Mowers, reapers, *ligarello*

And *rastelarello* [6], all, and mustered
At the homestead. On the grass-grown
Treading-floor the master sat
His wife beside, the Muster of the hands
Awaiting silently. The people
Marvelling at being called off
From their tasks, said on arriving, Master,

Thou hast sent for us and here we are.
The great storm always comes in harvest,
Master Ramoun raised his head and said;
However well-advised we may be
But poor creatures we are all, aye stumbling
On misfortune. Tell me now, good friends,
What each knows and what each has seen.

Laurèn de Gòut [7]
Forward steps. He never from a child
Had once failed with his sickle quivered,
When the corn-fields yellowed, to the plains
Of Arles to find his way. Brown as a church-stone
Was his skin, and he as strong
As an old rock the sea has vainly battered

With its waves. The sun might scorch
Or the *mistral* might blow,
But this old captain of the sickle
Ever was the first at work.
The reapers had elected him their chief.
Began Laurèn de Gòut:
God arrest the earthquake!

Master presages us tears; of this
We may be sure as that it rains or snows
Whene'er the dawn is ruddy.
As the light this morning night was driving
Westward, wet with dew as usual,
We beginning were when, Comrades!
Cried I, let's about the work go

Properly, and with a will. Accordingly
I tuck up sleeves and gaily to my task bend.
Master, lo, at the first stroke I cut myself!
For thirty years it, *bèu Bondiéu!*
Hadn't happened to me. Then he showed
His fingers bleeding from a deep gash.
Seeing which Mirèio's parents groaned

More heavily. Jan Bouquet, mower, knight
Of Tarascon, of *La Tarasque* [8], a fine youth,
Rough but kind and friendly, was the next
To speak. Ah! none so well as he
And with such grace in Condamino [9]
Waved the javelin in the air,
When the old witch, Lagadigadèu,

Ran the streets through, and the gloomy town
With dances brightened up and rang
With noisy mirth. He would have ranked
Among the masters of the scythe had he
To duty's path kept in the pastures. But
When holidays came round, adieu the scythe!
He was a roisterer, a very Thraso·

At the revels in the arbour,
At the orgies in the vaulted tavern,
In the interminable *farandole*,
And at the bull-baits. Thus began the youth:
Master, as we were mowing with long sweeps
I spied a nest of francolins beneath
A tuft of tares. They were their half-fledged pennons

Fluttering, and I gaily stooped to count them.
But, O fatal luck! poor little animals!
Some frightful red ants had possession got
Of nest and little ones. Three were already
Dead. The rest infested with the vermin
Stretched their piteous heads out of the nest
As if to say, Oh! come and save us!

But a cloud of ants more venimous
Than nettles, furious eager greedy,
Were upon and stinging them. While I,
All pensively incumbent on my scythe,
Afar the mother heard bewailing them.
This tale of woe to father mother
Was a lance-wound, tending to confirm

Their worst presentiments. Then as
The tempest gathers silently in June,
Over the plain the weather lowers,
Clap follows clap, and the north-east [10] is lit
With lightning; lo, Lou Maran comes!
On winter-evenings, when the stallëd mules
Drew lucern from the racks,

Oft would the ploughmen, speaking of the day
He came for hire, the oil in their lamps
Exhaust. It was at seed-time.
All the plougmen had begun to trace
Their furrows, save Lou Marran,
Who remained his tackle, coulter, ploughshare,
Eyeing as though he the instrument

Had never seen before. At last
The ploughman-chief assails him, Lout!
You plough for wages! Why, I'll bet
A hog would with his snout plough better. Done!
Says Marran, and whichever, master, loses,
I or thou, three golden louis loses.
Blow the trumpet! They two lofty poplars

Take for goal. The ploughshares cleave
The stubble, never from the straight line swerving,
While the sun both ridges brightens up.
Rampau de Dièu [11] *!* cried the men at once,
Thy furrow is, O chief, the furrow
Of a man of valor. But and nothing but
The truth to tell, so straight the other is

That verily one could throughout its length
An arrow shoot. Lou Marran won the wager.
In the parliament assembled he,
Trembling all over, pale, his bitter word
Deposed as follows. As I was, said he,
Awhile since whistling o'er the share ;
The ground is hard, thought I, the day we'll stretch

A bit to finish off. When lo, I see
My two beasts bristle up their hairy coats,
Lay back their ears, with horror quake, and stop short
Then and there. I saw the field-herbs
Bend down even with the ground, and fade.
I touch my beasts. Baiardo sadly
Looks at me, but never budges. Fallet

Snuffs the furrow's ridges. With my whip
I lash their shins. They start off scared.
The beam, an ashen one, is shivered to bits.
Tackle and yoke are carried off. And I,
Oppressed and pale, was seized as with a fit
Of epilepsy. With involuntary
Strong convulsion my jaws ground.

I felt Death like a gust of wind
Pass over me. On end my hair stood
Like a thistle!
The afflicted mother here cries desp'rately
Bono Maire de Diéu! with thy mantle
Cover my sweet child. And as she
On her knees, with face to heaven turned,

Again was 'bout to speak, behold Antèume,
Shepherd-chief and milker, comes up with long stride
And mutt'ring, What possessed her to so early
Rise and haunt the junipers? then entering
The council he as follows spoke:
Master, the welkin over the vast plain
Was still all hobnailed with the stars of God,

And we beginning were to milk the sheep,
When lo, a soul, a spectre or a shadow,
Flits across the path! The dogs are mute
With fright. The sheep together huddled.
If a good soul you be, speak to me!
If not, then to the flames return!
Thought I, who never have at Nostro Damo,

Master, leisure for an *ave*. Then
A well known voice cried, To the Holy Marys
Will no one among the shepherds
Go with me? And in an instant
She had vanished. Wilt thou credit it,
O master, 'twas Mirèio!
Is it possiblé! they all exclaimed at once.

It was Mirèio, I affirm it!
Cried the shepherd-chief; I saw her
In the starlight sweep by me.
I tell you verily I saw her.
Not as once she used to be,
But with her wan scared face, by which
On earth we knew some heavy grief oppressed her.

With a groan the laborers grasp
Each-óther's horny palm.
The stricken mother cries, O young men,
Take me over to the Saints! I must,
Wherever she has flown to
Follow my sweet bird, my partridge
Of the stony fields. The ants!

Should they attack you, to the last
My grinders grind them shall, ant-hill and all!
Should gaunt voracious Death
To twist you venture, I will jog
His old worn scythe, and you'll flee through the jungle
Wildly thus raved Jano Mario
As they through the fields returned,

Beside herself with apprehension.
Now the master speaks. Set up the cart-tilt,
Cartman; grease the axle, wet the nave,
And sharply put Moureto [12] to,
For it is late and we have far to go.
Into the cart gets Jano Mario,
And the air is more than ever filled with

Her delirious, plaintive, transports.
Lovely darling! Stony wilderness
Of Crau! vast salt-plains! you great sun!
Be loving to my drooping daughter.
As for the abominable Witch
That wheedled to her den my child,
And most assuredly poured out for her

And made her drink her potions
And her poisons; Taven! may the demons
Seize her, every one that terrified
St Anthony, and drag her over all
The rocks of Baux!
The poor unhappy woman's voice
Was by the noisy jolting of the cart

Now drowned. The servants of the *mas*,
One last look taking just to see if haply
Some-one from La Crau
Might not be coming,
Slowly to their work returned.
Musketoes swarmed, meandered humming.
Happy they!

NOTES

TO THE NINTH CANTO

.

1. — *Lunch*, a light meal reapers take about ten in the morning.

2. — *The scarlet-oak*, called by some *the holm*. *Quercus ilex*. — T.

3. — *Jean Althen*, an Armenian adventurer who, in 1774, introduced the cultivation of madder into the Comtat Venaissin (depart'. of Vaucluse). In 1850, a statue was erected to him on the Avignon rock.

4. — *The centaury-starred field*. *Centaury*, the solstice centaury, *centaurea solstitialis*, a plant that teems in the fields after harvest. Its yellow flowers and star-like prickles have suggested its Provençal name, *auriolo*, which means a halo.

5. — *The Provence cane (arundo vulgaris vel donax),* very common in Provence, whereof are made cattle-pens, angling rods, etc. — T.

6. — *Rastelarello,* female rakers. — T.

7. — *Gòut* (Goult or Agoult), a village in the department of Vaucluse, that has given its name to one of the most illustrious houses in Provence.

8. — *La Tarasque.* All the world has heard of La Tarasque, a monster that, according to tradition, ravaged the banks of the Rhône, and was destroyed by St Martha. Every year the people of Tarascon celebrate their deliverance by the exhibition of the monster in effigy; and at intervals of time more or less long the *fête* is enhanced by various games, such as that of the pike and the flag mentioned in the poem, which consists in gracefully waving and in throwing to a great height and catching with address a standard with large folds, or a javelin. *Lagadigadèu* is the *ritournello* of a popular song ascribed to king René, and sung at Tarascon at this *fête.*

9. — *Condamino,* la Condamine (*campus Domini*), the name of a certain quarter in Tarascon.

10. — *The north east.* The *tremountano* is the N. E. wind, and by extension the N. E.

11. — *Rampau de Diéu,* palm of God. — T.

12. — *Moureto* the name of the female, Mouret that of the male, animal. — T.

In the country beasts of burthen are usually named after their color. The most common names are *Mouret*, black; *Blanquet*, white; *Brunen*, brown; *Falet*, grey; *Baiard*, bay; *Roubin*, light bay.

MIRÈIO

CANTO X

CAMARGUE

Good people of Provence from Arles to Venço[1],
And from Valensolo to Marsiho[2],
Listen to me. While Mirèio
I sing, you pity Vincen.
Should you find the weather warm, friends,
We will to the Durençolo[3] banks
Repair and sit.

Managed by Andreloun, the little boat
The water cleft as noiseles as a sole.
The lovesick maiden I have sung
With Andreloun has ventured
On the Rhône, and sitting
Contemplates with vacant air the waves.
The boy says rowing, See how wide the Rhône is!

'Twixt Camargue and Crau, young lady,
Might be held fine jousts! That island
Is Camargue; it reaches far enough
To see the Arlesian river ope
His seven mouths. Some tartanes as he spoke
Were slowly moving up, like graceful swans,
The stream resplendent with the rosy tints

Of early morn. The sea-breeze swelled
The canvas of the crafts and urged them on
Gently before it, like a shepherdess
A flock of white lambs. Feathery ash-trees
And gigantic poplars grateful shade
Afforded to the river's bank. Around these
And their stouter boughs were twisted

Aged wild vines, with their fruit
In knotty clusters hanging. And the Rhône
Pursued his way majestically tranquil,
Seemingly profoundly sad at losing
In the sea his waters and his name;
Or weary, sleepy, like a tall old
Dying man, his *farandoles*

And symphonies regretting, and his palace
Of the popes at Avignon.
Meanwhile the lovesick maiden I have sung
Has jumped ashore. Walk on as far as you've
A road before you! cries the little man;
The Saints will lead you to their chapel straight.
Then he the sculls seized, backed with one,

And with the other pulled his boat's head round.
Mirèio, through the fire that June
Is pouring down, like lightning flies.
North south east west [4] she sees a plain immense;
Savannahs that present no limit
But the horizon; marshes, bitter prairies
Where, luxuriating in the briny air,

Black oxen and white horses freely roam.
For only vegetation at rare intervals
Some tamarisks, sodas, shavegrass,
Golden-herb and salicornes [5]; at times
A seagull; or a long-legged hermit,
Casting as he flies across the ponds
His shadow; or a red-legged chevalier [6],

Or hern with a fierce look [7], that proudly erects
His crest of three white plumes composed.
The heat begins to enervate the maid.
Her neckerchief she loosens. But the sun
Now rising to the zenith glares
Ferociously, and, like an Abyssinian lion
Ravenous for food, devours the desert

With a look. How good it were
To stretch oneself beneath a beech-tree here!
The radiance of the sunbeams simulates
The sparks from steel upon a grindstone,
Quivering as they fly; or swarms of furious
Hornets. Worn and gasping from fatigue
And heat, love's pilgrim has the pin withdrawn

That held her bodice; and her bosom, heaving
Like twin-billows in a limpid brook,
Resembles the *pancratia* [8] that expose
Their whiteness to the sea in summer.
Presently the scene its sadness loses,
And a rippling spacious lake is seen.
All round its shore

The ground is oozy. The phylleria
And atriplex [9] have grown in stature,
And a little grateful shade afford.
It is a heavenly prospect, a refreshing
Dream of Promised land. A town appears
Along the azure water, with a wall
All round it, having princely houses,

Fountains, churches whose tall steeples
Lengthen in the sunshine, suburbs;
Ships, *pinello* [10] with their snow-white sails,
Are entering the port; the wind is light,
The flags and oriflames play languidly
Upon the masts.
Mirèio from her forehead wipes

The abundant moisture and, A miracle,
Moun Diéu! is about to cry,
But she runs on, persuaded that the Marys'
Tomb is there. Alas! the more she runs
The more the picture changes, the illusion
Fades. Fantasti [11] had the subtile fabric
Woven with a sunbeam, and its tints

Had borrowed from the clouds. She notwithstanding
Follows it. Its flimsy stuff
Is now disturbed; it wavers, melts,
And like a mist evanishes.
Mirèio all alone, bewildered
By the heat, still goes on o'er the heaps
Of odious burning moving sand,

Over the large salt-crusted màrsh [12],
Dazzling, and crisp-baked by the sun,
And onward through the rushes, reeds,
And fenny-herbs, the home of gnats.
With Vincen in her thoughts she'd skirted
Long the Vacarés' salt-shore [13]; already
The white church of the great Saints she'd sighted,

Looming in the distance like a ship
Making for land. The beams of the relentless
Sun here pierce her forehead as with arrows.
Poor unhappy maid! she sinks down
By the sea, she falls death-stricken
On the sand. O Crau, thy flower is
Cut down! O young men, weep for her!

When in a valley, by the river-side,
A sportsman turtle-doves spies innocently
Drinking, others cooing,
Quickly through the bushes with his gun
He comes up ardently, and it's the fairest
Always that he pierces with his shot.
The poor child in a swoon lay stretched

Upon the beach. A swarm of gnats
Was passing by, who seeing her expiring
Without e'en a sprig of juniper [14]
To screen her from the burning verberation,
Plaintively the viol playing
With their little wings, they hummed out,
Get up quickly, pretty one! quick get up!

For the heat of this salt-marsh
Is too malignant. And they stang her poor
Hot hands and all her neck and forehead;
While the salt-sea-spray with bitter dew
Her face besprinkled. Groaning
She rose up, and crying, *I!* my head!
Dragged her slow way along, poor child,

From salicorne to salicorne,
Till at the sea-side Saints at last
She staggering arrived.
Then with her eyes suffused with tears
She cast herself down on the chapel pavement,
Damp with infiltration from the sea,
And ardently as follows prayed:

O holy Marys, who can into smiles
Change our bitter tears, incline
Unto my grief a ready ear.
For when you know, alas! my cruel pain,
All my load of care,
You'll pitifully·come
And side with me.

I am a maiden young and love a youth,
Handsome Vincen; him, dear Saints,
I love, I love with all my heart!
I love him as the stream meandering
Loves to glide; or as
The little fledged bird loves
To try his wings.

Yet they would have me to put out this fire.
Quenched it will not be! They'd have
Me rend the almond-tree in bloom!
O holy Marys, who can into smiles
Change our bitter tears,
Incline unto my grief
A ready ear.

Nor anxious mother, Crau, nor wilderness,
Nought arrested me; from far,
From far I've come in quest of peace.
I feel the sun's fierce rays upon my head;
Down they seem to come
Like thorns and red-hot nails
And pierce my brain.

You may believe me though, me Vincen give;
Gay and smiling we will both
Together come and see you here.
My temples then will cease to torture me;
Yea, my face now bathed
In tears of anguish will
For joy shine.

My father stern objects to link our fates;
But a trifle 'twere for you
To touch his heart, O Saints of gold!
Though hard the olive be the Advent wind,
Breathing only on,
Will mollify it to
The proper point.

The medlar, sorb, are both sour when they're picked,
Make one shudder; yet a wisp
Of straw strewed [15] serves to sweeten them.
O holy Marys, who can into smiles
Change our bitter tears;
Incline unto my grief
A ready ear.

What's this that dazzles me? is't Paradise?
Open is the church! with stars
Bespangled all the vault above!
O happy I! the Saints descend, *moun Diéu!*
Cloudless is the air;
To me they come, with light
All radiant!

And is it really you? O patrons fair!
Hide away the rays emitted
By your crowns or I must die!
Your voices call me? oh, do veil yourselves!
Weary are mine eyes!
Where is the chapel? Saints!
You speak to me?

Thus in an ecstacy, Mirèio
On the flags knelt gasping, half dead,
With her arms extended,
Her head backward lying,
And her eyes wide open seemed to see
St Peter's portal and the other world.
Her lips moved not. Her soul was rapt

In contemplation and her lovely face
Transfigured. As the day advances
With its gold to crown the poplar-tops,
The night-lamp's rays that light death's chamber
Pale and paler grow. And as at daybreak
Flocks disperse, so now the chapel's roof
And pillars all withdrew, to make-way for

The Marys, three divinely lovely women,
In white shining robes, descending
Out of heaven down a pathway
Glittering with stars.
One to her bosom pressed an alabaster vase.
Alone the star that lightens shepherds
On calm nights recalls

Her Paradisian brow.
The second her fair tresses lets become
The winds' sport, and advances palm in hand.
The third, still young, her dark complexion
Veils a little with her pure white mantle,
While the flashes of her gorgeous eyes
The diamond's surpass.

They reach the mourner. Over her they bend,
And speak to her. Their speech so soft is,
And their smile so loving, that the thorns
Of martyrdom bloom on Mirèio.
Poor Mirèio! say they, comfort take,
We are the three Judœan Marys;
Comfort take, we are the patrons

Of the stormy-sea-surrounded bark;
At sight of us the waves return to calm.
Now raise your eyes. That is St James' road.
We were together at the further end
E'en now, and looking through the stars
At the processions that on pilgrimage
To Coumpoustello [16] go on his, our son

And nephew's, tomb to pray.
We hearkened to the litanies the pilgrims
In the fields recited, blended with
The murmur of the fountains
And the peals of bells. In concert
All gave glory to our son and nephew,
Spain's apostle, sainted James the Major.

Happy at the glory thus ascending
To his memory, on the pilgrims' brows
We shed the dew of peace, and poured
Into their souls the oil of pure gladness.
Then it was your sad complaint ascended
To us ardently as flames of fire.
Your faith, O little maid, is of the sort

The great are constituted. But your prayer
Distresses us. From fountains of pure love
Foolishly you would drink, and foolishly
Before death you would try the strong life
Which we live in God himself.
Wherever found you here below
True happiness? Beheld it have you

In the rich man? Puffed up, cushioned,
Carlessly extended, in his heart
He God denies. But when the leech is gorged
It falls; and what will he do with his swelling
When he stands before the Judge who entered
On an ass' foal Jerusalem?
Beheld it have you on the mother's brow,

As with emotion to her infant she
Imparts her milk's first jet? One sup of bad
Suffices. O'er the cradle bending see her
Now, beside herself, her little dead-one
Covering with kisses.
Have you seen it on the bride's brow, as
With her betrothed she takes the path to church?

Go to, that path has more thorns for the couple
Treading it than has the sloe-bush of the heath;
For it is all besprent with trials and grave trouble.
The most limpid water here below
When drunk turns bitter. Here below
The worm is born with the young fruit, and all
To ruin falls or to corruption turns.

All vainly you may from the basket choose
The sweetest orange. Bitter 'twill
As gall become in no time. They who seem
To breathe in your world only sigh. But whoso
At a source unfailing incorruptible
Would drink, let him or her with suffering
Purchase it. The stone must needs be broke

To atoms for the silver-ore to be
Extracted. Happy therefore those
Who trouble take and in good works
Exhaust themselves, and who on seeing others
Weep, weep too, and who the cloak
From off their shoulders take to cover
Naked poverty, and who are humble

With the humble, and who stir for him
Or her a-cold their fire into a blaze.
The great word man forgets is, Death is life !
The meek the simple and the good are blessëd.
Favored by propitious gales, they wing
Their way to heaven quietly, and white
As lilies leave a world in which the saints

Are stoned continually. Could you, Mirèio,
See from the supreme Empyrean heights
How full of suffering is this nether world,
How foolish miserable all your ardor
After matter, and your churchyard-fears !
Poor lambkin, you would bleat for death and pardon.
But before the wheat can grow up

Into ear, it must within the earth
Ferment. Such is the law.
We too before we had our beams
Had drunk our bitter cup.
And now, that your faith fail not, we will
All our voyage's alarms
And tribulations tell you.

The Saints paused.
The waves to listen, coaxingly
Had flocked along the shore;
The pine-trees signs made
To the rustling reeds;
And to the wonder of the teal and ʃgulls
The Vacarés her bosom calmed.

The sun and moon adored,
Inclining their large crimson brows
Over the farthest marshes; and Camargue
Salt-saturated thrilled,
As the three blessëd Saints
To fortify love's martyr
Thus began.

NOTES

TO THE TENTH CANTO

———

1. — *Venço*, a small town in the department of the Var, not far from Antibes, formerly a see.

2. — *Marsiho*, Marseilles. — T.

3. — *Durençolo.* This name is given to the canals derived from the Durance. *Valensolo*, a small town in the L. Alps.

4. — *N. S. E. W.* The Provençal locution literally is from sun to sun and from wind to wind, meaning from east to west and from north to south.

5. — Tamarisk, etc. ; *tamarix gallica*, Lin. Soda, *salsola soda*, Lin. Salicorne, *salicornia fruticosa*, Lin. All plants common in Camargue.

6. — *A red-legged chevalier.* The Provençal name, *cambet*, designates several birds of the order of the

échassiers, chiefly the large red-legged chevalier, *scolopax calidrix*, Lin., and the small red-legged chevalier, *tringa gambetta*, Lin.

7. — A hern with a fierce look, *ardea nycticorax*, Lin.

8. — Pancratia, *campaneto* or *ile de mar* in Provençal. The author alludes to the beautiful flower, *pancratium maritinum*, Lin.

9. — *Phylleria* and *atriplex* ; *phylleria latifolia*, Lin., a large shrub of the family of the jessamine; *atriplex portulacoïdes*, Lin. (*Orage or, orach, golden-herb.* — T.)

10. — *Pinello*, sailing-boats. — T.

11. — *Fantasti*. See Canto VI, st. 38, and following.

12. — *The large salt-crusted marsh*, a vast sterile space covered with a saline incrustation due to infiltration from the sea.

13. — *The Vacarés*. See note 7 to 4th Canto.

14. — *Juniper* the *juniperus phœnicea*, Lin.

15. — *Straw strewed*. Medlars and sorbs are ripened on straw.

16. — *Coumpoustello*, in the middle ages, *Campus Stellæ*, erst the capital of Galicia in Spain, now a town of about 30,000 inhabitants, with a fine old cathedral containing the tomb of St James the Major, the patron Saint of Spain. — T.

MIRÈIO

CANTO XI

THE SAINTS

The Cross was standing, O Mirèio,
Damp still with the blood of God:
Over the city of the crime it cried, What hast
Thou done, what hast thou done, with Bethlehem's ki
Loud clamors from her streets no longer rose.
Cedron lamented him afar off. Jordan
Sorrowing pursued his desert-course,

And murmured mid the lentisks
And green terebinths his sad complaint.
And the poor people too were sad.
Full well they knew he was their Christ,
He who the door of his own sepulchre
Had forced; he who to his companions
And disciples had returned

To show himself; and who, the keys to Peter
Having left, ascended up to heaven
Like an eagle. Ah! they mourned in Jewry
For the handsome Galilean carpenter;
The fair-haired carpenter who all hearts won,
What with the honey of his parables,
What with his bounty to the multitude

In feeding them with bread unleavened
On the hills, their lepers cleansing,
And their dead restoring them alive.
But all the horde of traffickers the Master
From his holy temple drove, the scribes
The priests the kings, these muttered,
How restrain the multitude, unless

In Sion and Samaria the Cross' light
We speedily extinguish? And they raged,
And holy martyrs witnessed.
Stephen till he died was stoned.
Another, James, despatched they with the sword.
And others crushed were under blocks of stone.
But all on yielding up the ghost exclaimed,

Christ Jesus is the son of God!
Then us, the sisters and the brothers
Who had followed him from place to place,
They drove on board a crazy hulk
Deprived of sail or oar,
And to the fury of the sea consigned.
The men their eyes to heaven raised,

We women shed a flood of tears.
Receding we already mark the city,
Temple, palaces and towers;
Finally the Mount of Olives,
Carmel's crests and rugged sides.
When suddenly a voice is heard. We turn
And lo, upon the shore a maid.

She raised her arms and cried, My mistresses,
Oh! take me with you in the boat!
I too must die a bitter death
For Jesus' sake! It was our servant Sarah;
And you see her now in glory
Shining like an April dawn.
Aquilo far from shore was blowing us.

But lo, Salome, God-inspired, overboard
Into the water cast her veil. And now,
O mighty faith! upon the white and blue
Rough sea, the handmaid from the far-off shore
Our frail bark reaches, by Aquilo driven
And the veil upheld! Again we turn
Our faces landward, and as through the haze

We watch the hill-tops vanish one by one,
Till nought was visible but sea and sky,
Then the homesickness we were seized with
None can realise but those who've felt it.
Holy-land, adieu! Judæa doomed
To grief. For crucifying thine own God
And driving from thee thy just ones,

Thy vines, thy dates, the tawny lion's pasture
Shall become; thy halls the haunts of serpents.
Over the fearful sea
A storm of wind the vessel drove.
Upon the poop was kneeling Saturninus,
Also Martial. In his cloak wrapped round him
Sat, by bishop Maximin, old Trophimus

In meditation. On the main-deck
Lazarus was standing, with the mortal
Pallor of the grave and windingsheet
Upon him still. He seemed the stormy
Elements defying. By him was
His sister Martha and, crouched in a corner
Weeping, Magdalen. The hulk by demons urged

Contained besides, Eutropius,
Sidonius, Arimathean Joseph, Cleon,
And Marcellus. Leaning 'gainst the sides,
In psalmody they raised their voices,
And we all joined in *Laudamus te Deum!*
Oh! how the wretched bark toiled through
The sparkling waves! The whirling wind

Their crests stirred into foam. Out of the sea
The sun arose and in it set.
Day after day we wandered o'er
The vast salt-plain, the winds' sport ever.
Still from shoals and rocks God kept us free,
For he'd an end in view which was that we
Should under his law bring the Provence people.

Fine it was one morn above all others.
Night had fled before us lamp in hand,
Some early-rising widow like
Her oven going-to to turn her loaves.
The sea was smooth as any treading-floor,
And scarcely beat the sides. Anon we hear
A dismal moaning that with horror fills us.

And it louder grew. It seemed to issue
From the extreme horizon. 'Twas the wind!
It bore down on us rapidly. We watched
The waves dumfounded, scared; the sea about us
Crouched, was motionless and held the bark
The same as if by magic, ominously ;
While the blast swept formidably over.

Presently a liquid mountain rises
High and terrible, and the whole sea in heaps
With vapory sombre crests came,
O Lord ! rushing on us, and we
To the bottom of a gulf were
By a monster-wave precipitated,
Giddy, dying; then uplifted

By another to its summit.
Awfully the thunder burst;
The lightning cleft the darkness. Hell itself
Seemed loosed to swamp us. Roared and shrieked the
Oh ! what rough shaking, and what tossing !
On the shoulders of the sea we're raised,
Now to the abyss of darkness plunged,

Where sharks, seals, and sea-peacocks wander,
And alas! where the complaints
Of the poor sea-tossed drowned are heard.
A huge wave sweeps clean over us.
We're lost! My God! cried Lazarus,
Our tiller be! Once thou didst snatch me
From the grave. Send help, the bark

Is foundering! Like a woodpigeon
Did his cry for succour pierce the sky
And fly to heaven. Jesus saw him
From his elevation. Jesus sees his friend
Upon the raging sea, his friend
Who in another minute had been buried
In the same. His eyes beheld us

Tenderly, and all at once a lengthy
Sunbeam, *alleluia!* penetrates
The storm. Upon the water up and down
However we continue to be tossed
And harassed, and to taste the bitterness
Of sickness. But all dread had left us
With the clearing of the dense clouds,

With the quelling of the haughty waves,
And with the sight of green land through
The brightened weather.
Still the old hulk labored heavily.
At last her head is veered round
By some friendly breath, when like a grebe
She glides between the breakers and her keel

Ploughs up the froth in flakes.
She touches, *alleluia!*
On a rockless shore.
We cast us down upon the damp sand
And exclaim, Our heads that thou hast rescued
From the tempest ready are, we swear,
To preach thy law e'en to the death, O Christ!

At this new name with joy thrilled
The noble land of Provence, with her mountains
Forests plains and lakes; e'en as the dog,
Hearing his master's step, runs forth
To welcome him. A feast thou, *Pater noster*
Qui in cœlis es, hadst ready for us
After our long fast. The sea had thrown up

Shells; a spring among the salicornes
We found; the same that limpid wholesome
And miraculous still wells up
In the chapel where our bones repose.
By faith impelled at once along
The shingly Rhône we speed, then over moors.
At length we find with pleasure

In the land some traces of the plough.
Arles' towers we perceive surmounted
By the standard of the Emperors.
A reaper thou art now, O Arles! Reposing
On thy treading-floor thou dreamest
Of thy former glories with delight.
For then thou wast a Queen, and mother

Of so fine a race of rowers
That the wind could not the shipping
Of thy harbour traverse. Rome had newly
Clad thee in white well-knit stones.
She'd pranked thy suburbs with the six score portals
Of thy large Areno. Thou, princess
Of Rome Imperial, hadst thy pompous

Aqueducts, thy theatre and hippodrome
To while thy leisure hours away.
Now we the city enter. To the theatre
The crowd in *farandole* was going.
Thither we repair too. Through the shady
Marble-temples and the palaces
The throng of eager people rushes

Like a heavy rain-storm down
A maple-shaded deep ravine.
Oh, shame and malediction ! Bosom bare,
On the proscenium, ardently a troop
Of girls were dancing round a block of marble
They called Venus, to a chorus shrilly sung,
And by a lyre touched languidly

Accompanied. The people in their frenzy
Clamorously applauded them. Young men
And maids repeated, Let us the great goddess,
Venus, sing ; from whom all joy descends !
Venus the sovereign let us sing, the mother
Of the earth and the Arlesians !
And the idol, myrtle-crowned, with forehead

High, and nostrils wide distended, seemed
Amid the clouds of incense swollen with pride.
Old Trophimus, indignant at so much
Audacity, springs forward interrupting
Shouts and dances, and with outstretched arms
He, to the stupefaction of the crowd,
Arles people, listen! cries with mighty voice,

In Jesus' name! He said nó more.
But at the frowning of his shaggy brow
The idol staggers, groans, and headlong
From her pedestal is cast.
The dancers likewise prostrate fall appalled.
One howling cry is heard, the multitudes
Assemble at the gate, then throughout Arles

They spread dismay and terror. The patricians
Dash their crowns off, while the young men
Savagely rush on us with a thousand
Daggers gleaming in the air! But something
In a moment caused them to retreat.
Whether it was our salt-incrusted garments,
Whether Trophimus' now serene brow

Radiating holy light, or Magdalen
Veiled in a cloud of tears, more beautiful
A hundred times than their own stone-cold Venus,
Matters not; it possibly was all these.
Trophimus resumed. Arlesians, mark my words:
Afterwards you may kill me. You have just seen
Smashed like glass your god, at the mere mention

Of the name of mine. Ascribe not
To my voice this power, for we are nought.
The God that laid your idol low no temple
Has upon the hill, yet Day and Night behold
But Him up yonder. He alone' the earth
Created, he alone made heaven sea and hills.
His hand is mighty. Generous to prayer,

He is severe against all crime.
One day from his exalted dwelling, he
His property by insects saw devoured.
He saw the slave drink hatred with his tears,
And never one to, comfort him. He saw
In sacerdotal garments Evil keeping
School upon the altars, and your daughters

Running forth to meet the libertines.
To purge all this iniquity, to put an end
To the long suffering of pilloried
Humanity, he sent his own son, naked,
Poor, without array, into the flesh.
He sent him of a virgin to be born
Upon some stable-straw.

People of Arles, repent!
We the companions of his life
His miracles can vouch for. In the distant
Land where flows the yellow Jordan,
We in his white robe of linen saw him
Compassed by a crowd. Of God
He spoke to us as of a being all-good

And almighty; of his father's kingdom
Which for cheats usurpers and the haughty
Shall not be, but for the lowly, simple,
Those who weep. He told us we should
One-another love. His doctrine
He confirmed by walking on the sea.
The sick he made whole with a word, a look;

The dead, dispite the sombre rampart, life
Restored to. Lazarus behold,
Who in his windingsheet was rotting.
For such works and out of jealousy
The monarchs of the Jewish nation took him,
Led him to a hill, on to a tree's trunk
Nailed him, spat on him, heaped on him

Infamy with raillery, then raised him
Bleeding on the trunk into the air.
Oh, mercy! mercy! cried the people sobbing,
Mercy! What must we do to disarm
The Father's hand! Speak, man of God!
Say whether blood it is he wants? if so
A hecatomb forthwith we'll offer him.

Your vices, evil passions, immolate,
The Saint said, kneeling. No; what pleases thee,
O Lord, is not the odor of a butchery,
Nor temples built of stone. Thou lovest better
Far the crust presented to the starving,
Or the coming of the youthful virgin,
Sweet and timid, to present to God

16

Her chastity as 'twere a flower of May.
Thus from the great apostle's lips
The word of God like holy oil flowed.
And tears to trickle down, and sick and poor
And working-men to kiss his robe, and idols
Down the temple's steps to roll, began.
Sidonius then, the blind man born, bore witness,

Showing the Arlesians seeing eyes.
And Maximin the resurrection preached,
And the necessity of true repentance.
Arles that same day was baptized.
God's spirit bore us onward, like the wind
A fire of shavings. But behold, as we were
Leaving, comes an embassy imploring us.

One moment, strangers, sent to us from God.
Stay, listen. Hearing of your oracles
And miracles, our wretched city sends us
To your feet. While standing we are dead!
A monster prowls about our forest and ravines
Insatiate of human flesh and blood,
Sent by the gods to scourge us. Pity us!

A tail the beast has like a dragon's.
Redder are his eyes than cinnabar.
With frightful scales his back's all covered.
His large muzzle's like a lion's, and he has
Six human feet to run the better with.
His prey he carries to his den,
Under a rock that beetles o'er the Rhône.

Every day our fishermen, alas!
Grow fewer. Here the ambassadors begin
To weep. Without delay or hesitation
Martha cries, My mind's made up. We'll go,
Marcellus, to this people and deliver them.
For the last time on earth we all embrace,
And part in hopes of meeting happily

In heaven. Martial to Limoges repaired.
The spouse of Saturninus was Toulouse.
Eutropius was the first in pompous Orange
The good seed to sow. And thou, sweet Virgin,
Whither art thou going? Martha,
Bearing cross and holy-water, calmly
Marched against the monster, the Tarasco [2].

To behold the rare encounter
The Barbarians climb the pine-trees
Round the spot, ne'er dreaming she'd be able
To defend herself. Upon his litter
Roused, you should have seen the monster bound!
But 'neath the holy sprinkling vainly writhes he,
Growls and blusters, hisses!

Martha slips a halter made of moss
Around his neck, and leads him snorting out.
To worship her the people all run up.
Who art thou? great Diana? or the chaste
And wise Minerva? No, the maiden answered.
No, I'm but a handmaid of my God.
And then she taught them till with her they bowed

The knee to God. The rock of Avignon
She smote, but with her voice alone;
Whence forth gushed faith, and in such streams
That every heart consumed by sin
Ran to it for refreshment and forgiveness.
Clement and the Gregorys shall later
At it fill their chalices and drink.

Rome yonder for her glory trembled
Seventy years. How soon, when it has rained
A little, all the drooping trees and plants
Sprucely prick up their leaves. So soon did,
In Provence regenerate, ascend to heaven
Songs of praise, rejoicing to God.
Now notice her who's praying in yon grotto,

With her white arms tightly folded on her chest.
Ah! poor unhappy one! her knees are sore
With kneeling on the bare hard rocks.
For only clothing she her fair hair looses.
Lo, the moon with her pale torch is watching her.
To see her too the forest bends in silence.
Angels e'en restrain their beating hearts

And watch her through an interstice;
And when they spy a tear fall, quickly they
The pearl pick up and put it carefully
Into a golden cup. Enough, enough,
O Magdalen! For thirty years the wind's breath
Through the woods has brought thee thy Lord's pardon.
Yea, the rock henceforth shall weep thy tears,

And sprinkle, like a snow-storm, on
All woman's love their whiteness evermore.
But nought consoles the unhappy one,
A prey to sorrow: nor the little birds
On St Pieloun³ that flock to her for blessings
On their nestlings; nor the angels who
Seven times a day across the valley

Bear, and rock, her in their arms.
Marseilles the haughty, who thine eyelids openest,
On the sea, and from the sea deem'st nothing
Worthy to divert thine eye, and who
In spite of adverse winds of gold art ever
Dreaming, thou at Lazarus' word
Closedst thy lids and saw'st the night within thee.

In L'Huveaune ⁴, whose source the tears
Of Magdalen supply, before God
Thou didst wash away thy filth.
Again thine head thou'rt raising.
Ere the wind-storm blow remember,
On thy *fête*-days, how the tears of Magdalen
Thine olives water.

Once more tell us, hills of Aix, abrupt
Crest of Sambuque ⁵, old junipers, tall pines
That clothe the rocks of Esterel ⁶, and you
Mourven ⁷ of Trevaresso ⁸, with what joy
Your vales were filled when Maximin passed thro' them
Carrying the Cross.
O Lord, to thee is due all praise, and in

Thine entire splendor and reality
May we behold thee ever. We poor women,
By thy love touched, have of thy eternal
Glory some faint rays emitted.
To all ages, ye blue hills of Baux,
And Alpines, traces of our doctrine
Shall keep graved in' stone [9].

Death in the lonely marshes
At the bottom of Camargue, at last
Released us from our labors. As with all
That falls, oblivion soon had hid our tombs.
Provence however sang and time ran on.
And e'en as in the Rhône the Durance
Ends her course at last, so ends

The merry kingdom of Provence
By sleeping in the bosom of *La France*.
I'm dying, said her last king:
France, thy sister I commend
To thy good care. On the great work
The future has in store for you
Together counsel take.

Thou art the mighty, she the fair.
Heed me, and you shall see
Rebellious night before the splendor
Of your brows united flee!
One night, as in his featherbed he slumbered,
We revealed to René where our bones reposed.
With bishops twelve, his pages, splendid court,

And equipages, came the king
To this seashore, and found our graves
Under the salicornes. Time flies!
Adieu, Mirèio: we life flickering
In your body see, as in a lamp expiring.
Ere her soul its mortal frame quit, sisters,
We must to the heavenly hills repair

In haste. It's meet we should be there before her;
Meet and urgent. Her white robe and roses
We've to see to; for 'tis as love's martyr
And a virgin she's about to die.
Glory to Father, Son, and Holy Ghost!
Celestial avenues with flowers blow!
Empyrean's holy light shine on Mirèio!

NOTES

TO THE ELEVENTH CANTO

———

1. — *A Grebe*, a bird of the order of the palmipedes, *podiceps cristatus*, Lin.

2. — *The Tarasco*. See note 8 to the IX canto. — T.

3. — *St Pieloun*. See note 15 to VII canto.

4. — *L'Huveaune*, a small river that rises in the Sainte Baume mountain (Var), flows past Aubagne and reaches the sea at Marseilles near the Prado. A poetical legend ascribes its origin to the tears of S⁺ Magdalen.

5. — *Sambuque*, a mountain to the east of Aix.

6. — *Esterel*, a mountain and forest in the department of the Var.

7. — *Mourven*, the Phœnician juniper.

8. — *The Trevaresso*, a mountain-chain between the Toulombre and the Durance.

9. — It has been seen in the relation of the holy Marys that the bark of the proscribed Saints was cast upon the extremity of the isle of Camargue. These first apostles to the Gauls ascended the Rhône to Arles, and then dispersed over the south. It is even held that Joseph of Arimathea proceeded as far as England. Such is the Arlesian tradition.

That of Baux continues the Odyssey of the holy women. It states that they went and preached the faith in the Alpines, and to eternalise the memory of their doctrine, they miraculously carved their effigies on a rock. On the eastern side of the Baux rock this mysterious and antique monument may still be seen. It is an enormous upright block detached, and standing over the brink of a precipice. Upon its eastern side are sculptured three colossal faces, which are objects of veneration to all the neighbourhood round about.

MIRÈIO

CANTO XII

DEATH

As when God's day of labor ends
In orange-lands, the maids each-other help
To lift the heavy basketful on head or hip;
As when they 've lowered their nets, the fishers
Haul their boats up high beneath the rocks;
As when the golden clouds
Successively evanish; or as when

The far-off organ-peal, or hymn's last note,
Flits with the zephir over the old church;
As when prolonged harmonious the sounds
Of bleating goats, of shepherd's pipe, of songs
Of love, along the serpentining Argen's ¹ banks,
Over the hills and plains, along the lanes,
Crow gradually faint, and night

And melancholy take their place :
So fainter grew the ascending Mary's words,
Till they were heard no longer.
Sleeping, dreaming on her knees, she seemed ;
And a strange freak of sunlight crowned
Her brow with loveliness unwonted.
Thus it was her parents found her.

They had diligently followed her
Across the river and the wilderness ;
And, standing now beneath the porch,
They watch her in amazement.
Still or ever entering
They holy-water take and cross themselves.
The woman and the old man then

Over the sounding flags advance.
She, frightened as a yellowhammer
At the sight of fowlers, cries :
Moun Diéu! father, mother, whither
Are you going? then falls prostrate.
With her face all stained with tears
Her mother runs up, folds her in her arms,

Your forehead's burning, child! she cries ;
No, no, it's not a dream deceiving me,
It is herself! it is my child, my child!
And she together laughs and weeps.
Mirèio, darling, is is I, your father,
Rubbing these poor little hands so cold!
The old man wails out in his anguish.

But the wind by this time
Had the great news wafted through Li Santo [2],
And the church's porch was thronged
With anxious people entering.
Up to the upper chapel, shouted some,
The sick child must be borne to kiss
With dying lips our Saints' bones

In their reliquaries. Instantly
She's seized and borne off by two women.
Built with solid blocks of rock, three chapels
Superposed, with their respective altars,
Constitute this graceful church.
St Sarah is by the Bohemians [3]
Venerated in the chapel

Underground; the one above
Contains God's altar;
And the uppermost, supported
By the pillars of the sanctuary,
Is the funereal chapel of the Marys,
With its convex roof to heaven turned.
In this last are the relics : sacred

Legacies whence grace descends like rain.
Four keys the cypress-reliquaries lock.
Once every century they're opened, when
Thrice happy he who then can see and touch them !
Weather fair and lucky star his bark
Shall have; the tender branches of his trees
Shall basketsful of fruit bear,

And his soul, believing,
Everlasting blessings share.
A handsome oak-door richly carved,
Presented by the Beaucaire people,
This domain of sanctity protects.
But what especially protects it
Certainly is not the door that closes,

Nor the rampart that surrounds it, but
The grace by azure-space imparted.
Up the little turning stair, the sick-one
To the chapel is conveyed. The priest,
In surplice white, the door wide opens. Then,
As when a squall of wind shakes suddenly
A barley-field with heavy ears,

All on the dusty pavement fall and cry,
O handsome Saints! full of humanity,
Saints friendly, Saints of God! this poor maid pity!
Pity her! exclaimed the mother, Pity her!
And when she's well I'll bring you my gold ring;
My cross with flowers carved on it, and go
And spread the miracle through towns and country.

Master Ramoun groaned out, his head shaking
More than usual, Saints, she is my plover,
Saints, she is my treasure! Saints!
Here stumbling in the gloom, Send me,
Send my old bones to dung the mallows,
But my tender innocent! oh, spare her!
With closed eyes and speechless

Lay Mirèio. It was growing late.
And that the land-breeze
Might revive the *mas*-maid,
They removed her to the tiled roof
Opposite the beach, on which the waves,
Weary of chasing one-another,
Fall, and moanfully expire.

The landscape to the view presents
A boundless plain, one vast savannah,
Over which there stretches one immense
Blue sky, with nothing to indent the horizon
But some tamarisks that tremble
In the faintest breath of wind. Long fallows
Strewed with salicornes are seen,

And in the meres at their ablutions swans,
And oxen feeding on the sterile moor [4]
Or swimming o'er the Vacarés.
Some vague words in a feeble voice
Mirèio now has uttered.
Two breaths visit me, she said,
One from the sea, one from the land;

The one is fresh as morning air, the other
Fraught with bitterness is suffocating,
Ardent. Then was silent. All the Santen [5]
Turn them tow'rds the sea, then tow'rds the plain,
When they perceive a young man
Raising clouds of dust at every step.
The tamarisks to flee and dwindle seemed

Behind him. Vincen 'twas, the basket-weaver.
Master Ambroi had no sooner said,
My son, the pretty *falabrego*-spray
Is not for your lips, than he started off
To see her once again from Valabrego,
Like a bandit. Ah! poor lad
And worthy pity. He in Crau is told

She's to Li Santo gone. Nor tiresome Crau,
Nor Rhône, nor marshes, could arrest him
In his course. And when the church he enters
And beholds the crowd, he raises him
On tiptoe, deadly pale, and cries, Where is she?
Show me where she is! They answer:
Trembling in the agony of death

Upon the chapel's roof. Distractedly
The unhappy youth runs up, and when
He sees her, lifts his eyes and hands to heaven
And cries, 'Gainst God what have I done to draw dow
On my head such malediction?
Her throat have I cut whose milk I sucked?
Anathema! have I been seen to light

My pipe at a church-lamp? or Jew-like
Drag the crucifix through thistles?
Say, what crime have I committed
To be visited with all this wrath?
Malan de Diéu 6*!* it was not enough
That they refused her me, but they must
Martyrise her! Then he kissed her.

Seeing him take on at this rate,
All the pressing crowd his sorrow shared ;
They grieved at heart for him and wept.
The voices of the Santen, singing
The fine hymn they know, quaked like the hearts
Of shepherds when they hear the torrents
Rushing down the deep ravines. They sang :

I

O Saints, fair mariners, who chose
    Our marshes to erect
The battlements and tower on
    Of your white church, how shall
The troubled mariner direct
    His sea-tossed bark,

II

Unless you straightway send him wind
    And weather fair ? What shall
The poor blind woman do ? Nor sage
    Nor bugle in a case
So sad efficient is. Without
    A word her time

III

She passes, going o'er and o'er
    Her wretched life. To be
In darkness, darkness aye, is worse
    Than death. Her sight restore,
O Queens of Paradise ! And e'en
    As when the like

IV

Of us poor fishers humbly pray,
 You fill our nets with fish ;
So when heart-broken penitents
 For peace sue at your doors,
O white flowers of our briny moors, .
 Fill them with peace !

With cries heart-rending the good Santen prayed.
The Saints meanwhile a little vigor waft
To the poor prostrate sick-one, whose white face
Grew cheerful, even bloomed, at sight of Vincen.
Mine, she said, whence are you ?
Say, don't you remember at the farm,
When we were 'neath the trellis chatting,

You said to me, should misfortune
Overtake you, to the holy Marys run,
You'll surely get relief ? O Vincen dear,
What pity 'tis you can't see through my heart
As through a glass ! You'd see it
Overflowing with peace comfort happiness.
Lo, *lou bon Dièu* 's angel-choristers !

Mirèio here paused, gazing into space.
She seemed to see beyond the azure air
Things marvellous. Again she spoke :
O happy souls, that flesh no longer
Weighs to earth ! When they ascended, Vincen,
Did you see the flakes of light they scattered ?
What a precious book had been composed

Had all the words they said to me
Been written down! To weep unable
Vincen here his sobbing ceased and cried,
Oh! would to God I'd seen them,
Would to God I had!
I'd like a tick have fastened to their robes
And cried to them, O Queens of heaven!

Sole asylum left us! take from out
My head the eyes, my mouth the teeth,
From off my hands the fingers! but my pretty
Little fairy, leave her to me sound!
She, struggling to release her person
From her mother's arms and beckoning
With her hand towards the sea,

Now interrupts him with, They're coming
In their shining raiment! Instantly
All seaward turn, and shading eyes with hands,
We nothing in the distance can discern,
Say they, except the line at which the sky
Encounters the salt-water.
No, there's nought in sight. There is! there is!

Lo, there on board the sailless bark!
The waves before them, don't you see, lay down?
Oh! it is they! the air is clear,
And the breath balmy that impels them.
Yea, the very sea-birds do them homage
As they pass in flocks! The poor child
Is delirious: on the flushing sea

Is nothing but the sun about to dip
Within it. Yea, it *is* they! cried the dying child;
Go to, mine eye is not at fault.
O miracle of God! their bark is hither
Coming! To behold now she is
As a daisy the fierce sunbeams,
Ere 'twas fully blown, have burnt.

And Vincen horror-struck is crouching
By her side, and to the Saints,
To *Nostro Damo*, to the Saints
Of Paradise, her soul commends. The tapers
Have been lit. Girt with the purple stole
The priest with angels' bread comes to refresh
The burning palate of the dying maiden.

Extreme unction he administers,
And with the holy chrism in seven parts
Anoints her body, Catholic custom following.
Now nought is heard upon the tiles
But the *oremus* of the priest.
Against the wall the setting sun
His horizontal last beams casts,

And slowly come the sea's long waves
And dully break upon the beach.
Her tender lover, with her parents kneeling,
Hoarsely sobbed incessantly.
Again Mirèio speaks: The time of parting
Is at hand; quick shake hands! lo, the glory
Waxes on the Marys' brows; already

'Long the Rhône the rosy-hued flamingoes
Are assembling, and the tamarisks in bloom
Beginning to adore. O blessed Saints!
They beckon me to go with them; they whisper
I have nought to fear, their bark
To Paradise will take us straight, and they
The constellations know!

My little pet, if you should leave us,
Master Ramoun said, what will it serve us
To have rooted up so many dwarf-oaks?
All the ardor that sustained me came
Of you. The sun might burn, the heat
Reflected by the clods might parch me;
But the sight of you allayed both heat and thirst.

Good father, shouldst thou see a moth at night
Fluttering round thy lamp, it will be I.
But now the Saints are standing on the prow
Awaiting me. A little moment wait!
Yea, I am ailing, and move slowly;
This, oh! this is too much! burst the mother out;
I will not let you die! so stay with me

You must! Then, my Mirèio, when you're well again,
We'll go to aunt Aurano's with a basket
Of pomegranates: it's not far from Baux
To Maiano 7; in one day we'll go and come.
Not far, good mother? No, it's not.
Believe me though, alone thou'lt do the journey.
Mother, give me my white raiment:

See how splendid are the Mary's mantles!
Dazzling as the snow upon the hill-sides.
Here the swarthy weaver cried, My all,
My pride, my Empress! you who had your palace
Oped for me, and given me your love,
An alms in blossom 8*!* you who had my mire
Purified and brightened like a mirror,

And of ill-fame free hereafter
Rendered me! O Provence pearl,
O sun of my young life, shall it be said
I saw on you the beads of dissolution!
O great Saints, shall it be said that you
Within your sacred precincts saw her
In the pangs of death all vainly!

My poor Vincen, faintly answered him
The maiden, what have you before your eyes
So frightful? Death? death is deceptive.
What is it? A fog a knell dispels;
A morning dream that wakens us.
But I'm not dying! Light of foot
Behold, I've stepped into the bark!

Adieu, adieu! we're in the offing!
Now we're on the open sea; the sea,
Vast agitated plain that reaches
The blue firmament all round and leads
To Paradise. *I!* how the billows rock us!
· Yonder 'mong the many stars
I'll find some friendly hearts, and we'll be free

To love each-other. Saints! is that an organ
Playing? And the dying maiden sighed,
And laid her head as though to sleep.
One would have by the smile upon her face
Supposed her speaking still, had not the Santen
In a file approched the maiden
With a taper which they passed from hand to hand,

As each the cross' sign made over her.
The parents stupified beheld them.
Livid! Out upon it! Luminous they see her.
Vainly too they feel she's cold : they will not,
Cannot, in the dreadful blow believe.
But Vincen when he saw the forehead
Lying back, the arms quite rigid,

And the sweet eyes veiled, exclaimed,
She's dead! she's, don't you see, quite dead?
Then with his sleeveless arms gesticulating,
And his clasped hands wringing desperately,
Piteously he wails out, You'll be wept for!
But you're not the only one :
With yours the trunk of my life too has fallen.

Dead! she's dead? impossible!
Some demon must have whispered it.
In God's name speak, good friends here present.
You have seen dead women : tell me whether
Passing through the gates they smile so? Almost
Merry verily her features seem,
Now don't they? But what mean they with their faces

All averted? Sorrowing! Ah, this means,
I am never more to see her living;
Never more to hear her voice,
Nor listen to her pretty prattle more!
Here all hearts leapt and tears in showers fell,
And sobs heart-rending mingled
With the waves' sad moans.

Among a numerous herd of cattle
When a heifer dies, around her
Stretched-out carcase bulls and cows assemble
Nine eves following, all mournfully
To grieve for her, and make the plain,
The sea, the wind, resound for nine days
With their lamentable lowing.

Vincen went on: Poor old Master Ambroi!
For thy son thou'lt weep, alas, alas!
Good Santen, listen to my last wish: it is
That you take me with her to the grave;
For a like mourning tears are not enough.
Dig in the oozy bay one crib for both;
Around it raise a wall of stones, so that

The sea may never part us. Do, good Santen,
For me as I say; I trust to you.
Then where she dwelt, while they are
The floor battering with their foreheads for remorse,
We'll (she and I) in the calm azure lie,
Beneath the unrest of the upper water.
Yea, we'll lie, my oh, so pretty! side by side,

And you shall tell me over, over, over,
All about your Marys.
With your shells, O sea-storms, cover us!
The unhappy weaver here, his mind quite gone,
Himself upon Mirèio's body cast,
And clasped it franticly. Manwhile the hymn
In the old church continued to be sung:

So when heart-broken penitents
    For peace sue at your doors,
O white flowers of our briny moors,
    Fill them with peace !

THE END.

NOTES

TO THE TWELFTH CANTO

———

1. — *Argens*, a river in the department of the Var.

2. — *Li Santo*. See note 21 to the 1ˢᵗ canto.

3. — *The Bohemians*, the Gipseys. — T.

4. — *The sterile moor*. See note 12 to the X canto.

5. — *The Santen* (*li Santen*), the inhabitants of Li Santo.

6. — *Malan de Diéu*, evil year of God. — T.

7. — *Maiano* (*Maillane*), a village in the *arrondissement* of Arles, and the poet's birth-place.

8. — *An alms in blossom*, an alms that a poor man has received, and which he gives to a poorer; a poetical locution, equivalent to *a rare benefit*.

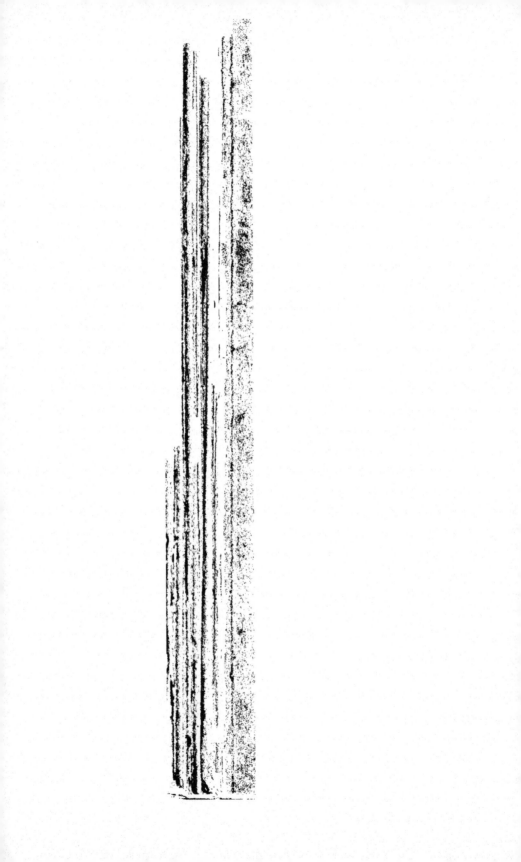

CPSIA information can be obtained
at www.ICGtesting.com
Printed in the USA
LVOW13s0016080717
540642LV00035B/1329/P